Studies in Writing & Rhetoric

Studies in Writing & Rhetoric

In 1980 the Conference on College Composition and Communication established the Studies in Writing & Rhetoric (SWR) series as a forum for monograph-length arguments or presentations that engage general compositionists. SWR encourages extended essays or research reports addressing any issue in composition and rhetoric from any theoretical or research perspective as long as the general significance to the field is clear. Previous SWR publications serve as models for prospective authors; in addition, contributors may propose alternate formats and agendas that inform or extend the field's current debates.

SWR is particularly interested in projects that connect the specific research site or theoretical framework to contemporary classroom and institutional contexts of direct concern to compositionists across the nation. Such connections may come from several approaches, including cultural, theoretical, field-based, gendered, historical, and interdisciplinary. SWR especially encourages monographs by scholars early in their careers, by established scholars who wish to share an insight or exhortation with the field, and by scholars of color.

The SWR series editor and editorial board members are committed to working closely with prospective authors and offering significant developmental advice for encouraged manuscripts and prospectuses. Editorships rotate every five years. Prospective authors intending to submit a prospectus during the 2002 to 2007 editorial appointment should obtain submission guidelines from Robert Brooke, SWR editor, University of Nebraska–Lincoln, Department of English, P.O. Box 880337, 202 Andrews Hall, Lincoln, NE 68588-0337.

General inquiries may also be addressed to Sponsoring Editor, Studies in Writing & Rhetoric, Southern Illinois University Press, P.O. Box 3697, Carbondale, IL 62902-3697.

Whistlin' and Crowin' Women of Appalachia

Whistlin' and Crowin' Women of Appalachia

Literacy Practices since College

Katherine Kelleher Sohn

With a Foreword by
Victor Villanueva

SOUTHERN ILLINOIS UNIVERSITY PRESS

Carbondale

Printed in the United States of America
09 08 07 06   4 3 2 1

Publication partially funded by a subvention grant from The Conference on College
Composition and Communication of the National Council of Teachers of English.

Library of Congress Cataloging-in-Publication Data
Sohn, Katherine Kelleher, 1946–
    Whistlin' and crowin' women of Appalachia : literacy practices since college /
Katherine Kelleher Sohn.
        p. cm. — (Studies in writing & rhetoric)
    Originally presented as the author's thesis (Ph.D.)—Indiana University of
Pennsylvania, 1999.
Includes bibliographical references and index.
1. Literacy—Kentucky—Case studies. 2. Women college graduates—Kentucky—
Language—Case studies. 3. Rural women—Kentucky—Intellectual life. I. Title.
II. Series.
LC152.K4S66 2006
302.2'244'09769—dc22   2005024371
ISBN-13: 978-0-8093-2681-5 (cloth : alk. paper)
ISBN-10: 0-8093-2681-7 (cloth : alk. paper)
ISBN-13: 978-0-8093-2682-2 (pbk. : alk. paper)
ISBN-10: 0-8093-2682-5 (pbk. : alk. paper)

Printed on recycled paper. ♻

The paper used in this publication meets the minimum requirements of American
National Standard for Information Sciences—Permanence of Paper for Printed
Library Materials, ANSI Z39.48-1992. ∞

To my deceased mother, Teresa Berry Kelleher, whose dream became my reality.

To the women of this study, whose wisdom changed my teaching.

To the eastern Kentucky community that has given my family and me roots so far from our homes.

Contents

Illustrations

Foreword

A tale of colors within whiteness.

For a few years, she had been raised within and among the white middle class of Cincinnati, Ohio. There's a picture of her, maybe six, seated in a fancy pink dress and a wide-brimmed straw bonnet, perhaps a dozen Easter baskets displayed before her. She knew privilege. And as such, she knew she was better than those people from across the river, the "hillbillies."

But there were contradictions.

She had been adopted. She knew that, knew that she'd been born in Kentucky, adopted when she was about a year old. When she was six, the person she knew as mother died, an appendectomy that had gone fatally wrong. A few years later, the man she knew as father remarried. New household rules, including being forbidden to play with two friends—one black, one poor white. More, the new mother has no desire to be the mother. The child moves to a boarding school for the privileged, then to the orphanage from which she had come a decade earlier, then to children's jail, though for reasons that no one would consider criminal. Despite the literacy of the elite boarding school, despite the Easter baskets, her origins remain. She is the only literate white girl of the Training Unit for Girls, reading Dostoevsky on the q.t. while others are just beginning to acquire literacy, the luckier ones, the more ambitious ones.

At eighteen, she is no longer a ward of the state. After a time in the black ghettos of Toledo, she decides to find her birth mother (with the help of her poor white friend she had once been forbidden to associate with). Eventually, she does find her mother, meets with her once, only once in her life, in the outskirts of Appalachia. She had been raised to disparage hillbillies only to discover she is one. Her mother was from Appalachia, a single mother, too poor—

despite jobs—to provide care for her daughter, to provide meals for her daughter, giving up her child so as to save her child.

Ten years later, the twice-orphaned, institutionalized, highly literate hillbilly who lived among poor whites and blacks (yet maintained the distinctive dialect of white privilege) moves to Seattle after working as a ranch hand in northern Idaho and eastern Washington. She meets a Puerto Rican man who, like her, struggles to understand the irrational:

Carol Villanueva, once Carol Bradford Peters (who said that given the choice between two men's names, she'd take the one of someone she loves and who loves her), once Patricia J. (Patty Jean?) Bennington (a name discovered only this year, when she had to find her original birth certificate under new rules for obtaining a passport).

My wife.

My partner.

White middle-class Appalachian from poverty to poverty.

Always kind of funny when Latino friends and others of color are surprised that I would have a "white wife." If only matters were so simple. We both often wonder at white people. Yet we're both racially white, somewhat. Latinos embody every color (to the point of a Peruvian president named Fujimoro or a family friend who speaks only Spanish named Ratcliffe). Something of the same is true of Appalachians, there being a group that might have been Turkish, might have been Portuguese: the Melungeons, whose features have an uncanny resemblance to Carol's. The life of the orphan opens all possibilities.

Then again, Appalachian is a color, even if not recognized as such. There's an Appalachian "look" and Appalachian ways: buck teeth or no teeth and freckles, laziness and loose sexual mores, inbreeding and in-fighting, and a disparaged dialect. Sounds like racism to me—prejudice based on stereotypes, bigotries that cannot be readily discarded through class ascension. Whereas white folks who cross the class system claim prior trades—a seamstress's daughter, a mill worker's son—folks of color always have the color as part of the "victory": a poor black family, a poor Puerto Rican family, a poor family from the holler. There's a racialization to Appalachia, something more than a class reference, something akin to "ethnicity." One of my daughters describes her "race" as "Portobilly," recognizing her heritages, recognizing the bigotries in both epithets—Porto Rican (which is how Americans named us for most of the twentieth century) and hillbilly.

Within rhetoric and composition, we have known some discussion of and by people of color. But discussion concerning Appalachia has been scarce. Until now. Kathy Sohn, the outsider who has lived in Appalachia for thirty years, tells us about some of the women of Appalachia—their strength, their courage, the ways in which their contexts can define them—and how all of this connects with literacy.

In what follows, Kathy Sohn, an accomplished and experienced teacher-researcher-scholar, relates the stories of three adult Appalachian women who decided to attend college despite poverty, no spousal sanction, other familial responsibilities, and inadequate preparation for college. In her telling she breaks through stereotypes, managing sympathy and the rigors of ethnographic distance simultaneously, and we learn about their literary acquisition despite ideology, bigotry, and economy.

Until I read *Whistlin' and Crowin' Women of Appalachia*, I thought of Appalachians as the color without a name ('cause they're not white, surely not the whites of "whiteness studies"). I thought of Carol as "a contradiction in stereotypes, not to be pegged." Both are still true. But now I wonder at a new stereotype that emerges from the points at which Carol, Lucy, Jean, and Sarah meet—the Appalachian literate woman as power, as voice.

Victor Villanueva

Acknowledgments

This section recounts the numerous people who have made my dream of publishing this book possible; I hope it also honors the Appalachian region whose people have made me and my family welcome these thirty years.

Every qualitative researcher knows that trusting participants ensure successful research, so I am thankful to the women in this study—Judith, Hope, Mary, Faith, Polly, and case study participants Lucy, Jean, and Sarah (pseudonyms)—for the gifts of their time, insight, and trust. They opened my eyes to the courage it took to enroll in Preston College (pseudonym), and after hearing their stories, I regretted that I did not recognize the extent of their sacrifice sooner. They have changed my teaching in countless ways.

Working on my doctorate would never have occurred to me had it not been for Victor Villanueva. In the rhetoric and comp program at Northern Arizona University in 1988–89, he taught me about ethnocentrism and racism in his inimitable way and encouraged me to fulfill my potential by enrolling at the Indiana University of Pennsylvania. I am grateful for his mentoring all these years.

Without the IUP's graduate faculty, the dissertation on which this book is based would have never materialized. The idea for the dissertation topic evolved during conversations with several faculty but most particularly with Gian Pagnucci, who challenged me to write about literacy in Appalachia as Shirley Brice Heath had done in the Carolinas. Barbara Hudson, my adviser, provided insights at every stage of the process. Carole Bencich directed the dissertation, never faltering in her belief in the importance of these women's literacy. I am grateful to these three for sitting on my proposal, comprehensives, and dissertation committees. Other IUP faculty and staff members contributed to the exhilarating doctoral journey: Don McAndrew, Dan Tannicito, Mark Hurlbert, Jeannine Heny Donna,

Mike Williamson, Ron Emerick, the now deceased Patrick Hartwell, and division secretary Cathy Renwick.

The seeds for publishing this book were planted by Dr. Mary Jalongo in the Writing for Publication class at IUP. After completion of my doctorate in December 1999 and based on her motivation, I sent query letters to several university presses and to Studies in Writing and Rhetoric. In August 2000, Dr. Robert Brooke, editor of that series, responded with a two-page, single-spaced letter, outlining several possibilities for publication. I thank Robert for his precision, thoughtfulness, and faith in this project as he guided it to publication. The comments of Beverly Moss, Pam Takayoshi, Smokey Wilson, Ginny Crisco, and other SWR readers helped me transform the dissertation into a manuscript. Finally, thanks to the numerous editors with whom I have worked at Southern Illinois University Press who have patiently and kindly assisted this new author in getting the manuscript ready to be published.

The colleagues I have met as a result of Villanueva's encouragement to become involved with the College Composition and Communication Conference in 1990 deserve thanks, most especially Cheryl Glenn and the 2001 James Berlin Outstanding Dissertation Award Committee, who affirmed the importance of these women's voices in composition studies, and Glenn herself, who has been tremendously supportive of this publication; Marilyn Cooper, who gave me the chance to publish portions of this book in *CCC* in February 2003; and Kim Donehower, whose dissertation on a North Carolina Appalachian community was my bible during the research and whose comments on specific sections of this manuscript since then challenged me to improve the content.

Audiences at professional meetings whose questions and observations about these women confirmed for me the universality of their tales of courage and helped me fine-tune my analysis deserve gratitude: CCCC 2001, Watson Conference 2002, Peanut Butter and Gender luncheon series at Berea College, Kentucky Teachers of English and Language Arts 2004, and CCCC 2004.

Preston College, which has employed me and my husband during our years in Appalachia, granted two sabbaticals to my husband, Mark, during which time I earned my doctorate. Thanks to the Preston College presidents, academic deans, and colleagues who have championed my efforts.

The Appalachian College Association provided the funds for completing the second draft of this manuscript, and though it has gone through two other revisions, I thank them for the award of the John Stephenson Fellowship for summer 2002. I am also grateful to my ACA colleagues with whom I confer regularly and who confirm the value of the small college setting for regional students.

Many other friends in and outside the region have contributed to the success of this book by reading the manuscript and engaging in conversations about the women: Leatha Kendrick, Linda Scott DeRosier, Debbie Meister, Christen Shukwit, members of the Pikeville Woman's Club Book Group, Steph Barnett, Felicia Mitchell, Dick Theis, Katie Vanderbrake, and numerous others. Finally, no adequate repayment is possible to my good friend and neighbor Connie Wagner for her endless gifts of reading and editing every word of the study, responding with global and local revisions, and keeping this outsider honest.

Fred and Frances Sohn, my beloved father- and mother-in-law, enabled me to get my doctorate; their quiet love and wisdom have undergirded me throughout the thirty-some years of our acquaintance. Mark's brothers and their spouses also deserve thanks.

Though getting my doctorate was one of the most jubilant moments of my life, it could never surpass the birth of my children, Laura and Brian, and the continuing joy they bring me as young adults. They listened, edited, and encouraged me during this project, becoming impatient when I periodically lapsed into negative thinking. Mark, my husband of over thirty years, deserves thanks for many reasons: he spent his last two sabbaticals where I could earn my advanced degrees; he offered his psychology background and research knowledge during this process despite his partiality for quantitative studies; he set me straight when I wanted to get off track; and he continues to love me with a steady hand and heart.

Finally, I am thankful for the faith and support of my seven siblings and of my father, Leo Kelleher, whose Irish ancestors mined

xx   **Acknowledgments**

coal in Pennsylvania when they came to this country. His gift of the blarney and of openness to the integrity of each person he meets appears to be "in the genes." To my mother, Teresa Kelleher, I am grateful for the years she pushed me to have what she could not attain, a college education, and who, though she did not live to call me Dr. Sohn, dying six months before I completed the process, supported me with incredible insights during the research process. I think she would have been pleased to read these women's stories.

Whistlin' and Crowin' Women of Appalachia

Introduction

When the Conference on College Composition and Communication (CCCC) met in Nashville in 1994, I overheard two conferees refer to the strong southern accent of their server at breakfast and then launch into a few redneck jokes: "How to tell you're a redneck: You go to a family reunion to pick up dates. Your truck has nicer curtains than your trailer," and others. Having been raised in the South, I usually get pretty angry when I hear this kind of prejudice against people because of their dialect, birthplace, or class. I become especially incensed when the ridicule occurs among educated people like these two composition teachers, who, if asked, would probably pride themselves on their multicultural awareness.

Ironically, my CCCC presentation that year asked if rural working-class white folks might not need to be considered part of the multicultural community; I believed that this "color with no name" (Villanueva, personal communication) or "the white underclass, minority within the nation's white majority" (Purcell-Gates 2) was being left out of multicultural conversations. Without taking away from the concerns of people of color and ethnicity, I wanted to raise the awareness of compositionists about rural whites who are frequently the target of such jokes based on stereotypes that

> dehumanize . . . [and] ignore history, politics, economics, and culture [and] deny full humanity . . . serv[ing] to dismiss legitimate complaints about discrimination and to deflect potentially disturbing questions about who has money and power, who doesn't, and why. (Shelby 158)

I take comfort in the thought that this humor might have arisen out of the conferees' discomfort of being in another culture and that

1

these two comp people would be nothing but empathetic if the waiter were in their classes seeking to improve her lot.

Living in Appalachia since 1975, I wondered what my adopted neighbors would say to those making fun of them. Most likely, they would use their rhetorical skills to tell them a story with a clever ending to point out the ignorance of such jokes, but they would tell it in such a subtle way (my good friend, Herb E. Smith, calls it "deviling the opponent") that the jokesters would have to listen closely to get their point (personal communication). My Appalachian friends might themselves laugh at those redneck or hillbilly jokes if they told them about their own families, because good and bad stereotypes build group solidarity, but they surely don't want outsiders to tell jokes when those outsiders have no idea what they are talking about.

The Appalachian Region

People coming to the South or to the Appalachian region may come with attitudes like the CCCC conferees because of the way literature and the media have depicted the region. For a hundred or more years, the area has evoked fear with the dark images in *Deliverance* and the stereotyping of family relationships with the Hatfield-McCoy feud. At the same time, the region has been idealized with the depiction of women as earth mothers quilting, singing ancient ballads, or playing dulcimers, or it has been identified as the last bastion of the pure white Anglo-Saxon race (Billings and Blee). Finally, the region has been held up to ridicule for many years, most recently with a proposal by CBS in 2003 for a *Beverly Hillbillies* reality television show. These perceptions hold the region's people at arm's length because they do not measure up to some outside standard; outsiders make jokes to have some group on which to place their insecurities (Billings, Norman, and Ledford). Yet, the needs of the Appalachian people are no different from elsewhere, the need to be respected for who they are and for what they bring to the multicultural table. Like any marginalized group, they request the "etiquette of equality," which asks that they "be treated as equals . . . regardless of economic and social status" (Fiene 53).

Defining any region like central Appalachia is difficult because no place is monolithic. Though cultural regionalists "recognize a distinctive 'upland' culture subregion dominated by the foothills and mountains of Appalachia based on its unique 'cultural' landscape and individuals' cultural 'self-consciousness,'" the political boundaries of the Appalachian Regional Commission (ARC) identify the mountain range from Coharie County, New York, to Kemper County in Mississippi (McCauley 3). The term "Appalachia" most commonly refers to the central region, which contains portions of Kentucky, West Virginia, and Tennessee, "the smallest, poorest, and least populous subregion" of the ARC (Wood and Bischak; Isserman). Others say that boundaries of the region are mythical (Still), so much so that scholars describe the region as "invented" by outsiders and internalized by some insiders. These mythical borders have justified mainstream religious, political, and social programs to uplift the people and to counter illiteracy and poverty, setting Appalachia apart from mainstream America (Batteau; Billings, Norman, and Ledford; Jones, *Faith;* McNeil; Shapiro). Not having a realistic picture of the region and seeking to change rather than to understand the culture, they often did (do) more damage than good (Shapiro; Whisnant). Like the CCCC attendees above, even enlightened academics automatically connect illiteracy to Appalachia, most notably James Moffett, who "describe[s] Appalachians' illiteracy 'problem' as 'agnosis'—willful ignorance" (Donehower, "Literacy" 341). (See figure 1, a map of the region at the time of this study.)

Though outsiders may use the term "Appalachian," my Appalachian neighbors and the women in this study do not use it to describe themselves and would more likely explain their origins in terms of the holler, town, or county where they live. When I asked the women in this study to define the area, they responded with the reasons why they remain: seclusion from big city violence; improved roads and modest growth, which they define as both good and bad; and, primarily, close families and neighbors.

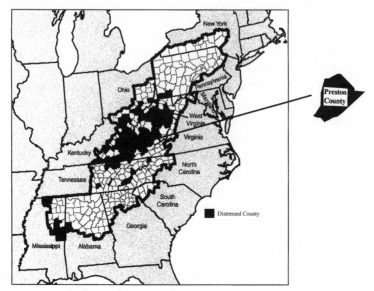

Fig. 1. Map of the Appalachian region: Distressed counties, 1998. (Compiled from U.S. Bureau of Labor statistics unemployment data, 1995; U.S. Census Bureau poverty data, 1990; and U.S. Bureau of Economic Analysis income data, 1996.)

The Research

What I found from this study opened my mind, heart, and teaching, especially to the importance of class in multicultural discussions of literacy. This narrative contributes to the plethora of "little narratives," other literacy studies that illustrate specific uses of literacy in many contexts and for many purposes, studies whose results are not meant to be generalized but which offer insights on literacy practices of different cultural groups (Daniell, *Communion* 4). Acknowledging that stereotypes such as those of the CCCC conferees arise out of ignorance, I thought that writing about the women in the Appalachian region would add knowledge about a population not often written about in composition literature to illustrate the "actual lived experience of members of marginalized groups in the United States, especially those [with] limited economic and educational options" (Guerra 5).

In chapter 1, I present the methodology of the Preston County study to demonstrate how I arrived at my findings. I describe the individual women involved in this study, comparing them to Appalachian flora to illustrate that this research is primarily based on individuals, whole women, who contribute to the general findings rather than being overshadowed by them. The chart at the end of the chapter provides a blueprint for identifying the participants in the remaining chapters of the book. (See table 2.)

Chapter 2 situates the women's stories within the context of theory, voice, and place. "Whistlin' and crowin'" relate to voice, a metaphor developed in *Women's Ways of Knowing* to "depict their [women's] intellectual and ethical development, and [to show] that the development of a sense of voice, mind, and self were intricately intertwined" (Belenky et al. 18). The women's search for self paralleled my own, so I begin this section by relating my voice to theirs in terms of language, identity, and power. Specifically, this chapter reveals how the women moved from silence to voice to identity by maintaining their dialect throughout college and beyond, by discovering the power of expressivist writing and completing their degrees to enhance their identity as strong women of Appalachia, by gaining economic and social power, and by remaining in their communities.

Place figures strongly in these women's identity. Because they are the cement of the Appalachian culture in spite of the appearance of a patriarchal society, the women shape the region as it shapes them. To illuminate the stage on which their literacy plays out, in the remaining part of chapter 2, I broaden the picture of life in eastern Kentucky in the central Appalachian Mountains by contrasting the region with the city my husband and I moved from over thirty years ago in terms of family, religion, economics, and culture. The women's words, my own as an assimilated outsider, and the words of Appalachian scholars represent as closely as possible what factors influence literacy and how the women use literacy for their own purposes.

The region provides the platform for the narratives of Lucy, Jean, and Sarah, which are the heart and soul of this monograph, in the chapters on literacy practices. Based on their own words interspersed with commentary and divided into the stages of pre-college,

college, and post-college literacy, each woman's story illustrates literacy practices as discovered in this study and supplemented by information from the five other women who took part in the first interviews.

One of the major findings of this study relates to the two-edged nature of literacy, described in chapter 3 with the story of Lucy and her abusive husband, who never allowed written materials in the house and made her keep her textbooks in the car. Lucy's story made me aware of outside pressures on working-class students and inspired my deepest admiration for women like her who persist in achieving a college degree to escape abusive situations. Not working outside the home at the time of this study, Lucy contributed to the community with art, sewing, poetry writing, letters to the editor, activities with her children, and expert help for her family and neighbors in their times of trouble.

Another major finding of this study was the continuing importance of formal and informal education once the seeds of success with academic literacy were planted, represented in Jean's case study in chapter 4. Poorly prepared for college, Jean overcame academic insufficiencies to graduate from college. Her persistence and motivation had moved her beyond her nursing degree to success in continuing education programs and a desire to complete a correspondence master's degree in critical care nursing.

Sarah's case study in chapter 5 demonstrates the intergenerational effects of literacy, beginning with comments from her mother and herself. Knowing that success in school generally depends on social class "origins [which] are more powerful in determining success" than academic or other factors (Knox, Lindsay, and Kolb 13) and that most of the study participants' parents had not completed high school, let alone attended college, I was amazed at the encouragement that these women received, mostly from their mothers like Sarah's Naomi. Continuing the intergenerational chain, the Preston County women had hoped that their children would attend college at the traditional age, so the chapter explores some evidence from the children who had graduated from high school at the time of this study.

These whistlin' and crowin' women taught me about coming to voice through college literacy. As a newly aware teacher, I offer in the conclusion suggestions to faculty and college administrators about ways to respond to nontraditional students; they are excellent resources on our campuses, but they have special needs. What these women taught me is that, while I am doing a good job, I can work to balance departmental emphasis on curriculum and proficiency exams with students' needs and concerns. As an educator, I can advocate for students through conferencing, advising, making referrals where merited, and listening to the messages I missed when I was teaching these women. Perhaps then I will hear their wisdom, learn from them, and challenge them to master academic literacy, whereby they can bridge the gap between the "motherwise" skills and knowledge they bring to the classroom, the "schoolsmart" skills they need to acquire (Luttrell), and finally the literacy skills they will need beyond college.

Though these women reside in Appalachia, their stories resonate with women like them across the nation who are isolated economically, societally, geographically, and culturally yet who manage to surmount obstacles to become self-fulfilled. Building on their survival skills, their education offered them personal growth, job advancement, and social empowerment, making life better for them and their children and thus enriching the Appalachian region. In this study, they taught me as a person and compositionist about strength, courage, and faith as they used their innate intelligence to "step out of safety" (Spellmeyer) by coming to college.

In particular, their whistlin' and crowin' voices might awaken other educators, as they did me, to the value, dignity, and worthiness of all students in the classroom. For their most significant gift to me, besides their unfathomable trust, was that they shocked me into looking at my class biases that I had glibly buried in my liberal humanist rhetoric, oblivious of the "long-established forces at play that maintain bigotry, systemic forces that can even make bigots of those who are appalled by bigotry" (Villanueva, *Bootstraps* xiv). I hope that my research helps to "make visible the complexity of local, everyday, community literacy practices and challeng[es] of dominant stereotypes and myopia" (Street, *Literacy in Theory* 7) as I was challenged.

What follows is the treasure of the whistlin' and crowin' women of Appalachia. Although education does not always deliver on its promise to transform lives (Gee; Street, *Literacy and Development*), my research reveals that it gave these women the ability to be heard in their homes, jobs, and communities as professionals—teachers, social workers, nurses, and experts in local affairs—achievements that built on their innate intelligence coupled with their college degree.

1 / The Preston County Study

Components of the Study

Setting

My primary purpose in conducting this research was to determine how going to college had changed the literacy habits of former non-traditional, working-class women and to ascertain how they were using literacy in the workplace, home, and community. A common aphorism submitted by students in the dialect unit I teach in fresh-men composition, "Whistlin' women and crowin' hens, always come to no good ends," appeared to be a useful metaphor or theme to carry through my study, since the self-confidence of these women might be compared to whistlin' and crowin' or coming to voice. Their stories would inform me whether their taking steps out of their cultural roles in this patriarchal society led them to good or bad ends.

All eight women lived in Preston County (pseudonym) in east-ern Kentucky, the largest geographic land area in the state bordered by West Virginia and Virginia. The county lies in a narrow valley situated amid rugged and steep mountains that allow little flat space for building, and the women often lived in trailers or houses sur-rounded by their families, up and down the hollers and creek bot-toms in places like the Right Fork of Rockhouse, Greasy Creek, and Stone Coal. Like the locals, the women frequented Preston, a town of 6,000, to renew their licenses, pay their bills, employ attorneys, shop at Wal-Mart or Lowe's, or eat at fast-food or retail restaurants.

The primary research site was Preston College (pseudonym), though this study was not classroom-based. The four-year liberal arts college from which the women graduated is located on a hill in the middle of Preston, which is situated in a county with a population of 75,000. The ninety-nine steps (and in 1998, an elevator) leading from the center of the town to the campus signify the literal and figurative journey the women took to go to college. Founded by religious missionaries, this private, Presbyterian college has served the Appalachian region with a Christian emphasis in higher education for over 100 years. At the time of the study participants' attendance, 90 percent of the undergraduate enrollment of 800 came from within a 100-mile radius of the college, and 96 percent were receiving some sort of financial aid ("Financial").

Selecting the Women

Because I had greatly admired them for their fortitude and determination when they had been students in my classroom, becoming reacquainted with these working-class, native-born Appalachian women who were the first generation in their families to attend college was a joyful experience for me. To select participants for the study, I examined old class lists and chose women based on their fulfillment of four criteria. Because I wanted to challenge stereotypes about Appalachian women being ignorant, I chose women who were Appalachian-born for two or more generations. Since the women had constantly mentioned in class how they hoped they were modeling education so that their children might come to college after high school, I also chose women who were married or divorced with children. Next, I wanted to recruit students who had been in my classes since I had completed my master's in rhetoric and composition at Northern Arizona University in August 1989 because my one year of teaching prior to that point was based on my twenty-year-old undergraduate English degree. Although I had originally planned to include women who had dropped out for one reason or another, my committee suggested the strength of interviewing graduates because the focus would be on more observable literacy practices based on a completed degree, which may or may not have changed their lives. Interviewing those who had dropped out would focus on other issues.

I came up with a list of thirty-four women, which I narrowed to seventeen by using only nontraditional Appalachian-born students and considering the availability of addresses and phone numbers from the Preston College Alumni Office. I eventually decided on eight participants based on my conversations with linguist Michael Montgomery and my perusal of the research of Virginia Seitz, Kimberley K. Donehower, Thomas Newkirk, Lorri Neilsen, and many others. In relationship to "purposeful rather than representative sampling" (Lincoln and Guba 102), I would describe the sampling as typical rather than atypical cases.

These eight women ranged in age from early thirties to midforties and graduated between May 1993 and May 1997, with five of the eight choosing education majors (reflecting the overwhelming choice of the women attending Preston College in the 1990s next to nursing); the remaining three majored in art, nursing, and psychology/human services. The time between high school and college ranged from seven to twenty-four years. They were raised in families that included only one child to those with six, seven, and nine children. All families were working-class, and none had collegeeducated parents. I chose married or divorced women with children because of the beliefs articulated in *Women's Ways of Knowing* that mothering "has as its center the teaching of the next generation," shaping women's ways of thinking and impacting their children (Belenky et al. 13).

After initial interviews with these eight women, I looked at several criteria to determine which three to choose for case studies. To allow for some time to measure literacy practices since college, I examined their time out of school since graduation, from four to six years. A representation of their school achievement, defined by their performance in class and overall GPA, enabled me to more adequately represent a broader picture of literacy than if I had interviewed only excellent students. For variety also, I wanted a representation of employed and unemployed women. And last, I chose the final three women based on the sheer personal interest I had in their stories.

After the remaining interviews, I asked each woman to read her transcripts for validity. In addition, I involved two native-born, college-educated Appalachian women to assist me in my research. Tina not only transcribed the tapes for me but also spent hours discussing how to record mountain dialect and what to include in the interview transcripts. In addition, my neighbor, Connie, a native of the region for many generations, acted as informant, editor, peer debriefer, naive observer, and outsider in the professional sense by editing every word of the dissertation, sharing observations about local as well as global issues, and confronting me with my biases. These remarkable women became informants and responders and verified the research data.

Positionality

A strong asset of qualitative researchers is their willingness to confront the biases they bring to their studies. My biases were many.

Though I was born a southerner who has felt prejudice from some who consider a southern accent either as a lack of intelligence or as a sign of cuteness, I identify with Appalachians and others marginalized by outsiders for accent and dialect, but I had to watch that my defensiveness did not lead me to inaccurate conclusions.

As a nontraditional doctoral student, I struggled with uncertainty and unfamiliarity with academic discourse, so I identified with the fears, adjustments, and successes these women encountered by coming to college at a nontraditional age. Similarly, we shared roles as women, wives, and mothers, so I was able to empathize with struggles to keep their families together while they worked toward improving themselves. Although both of our experiences exemplified how lifelong the literacy learning process is and how family pressures interfere, our experiences were different because of class and education.

Another factor to examine was my position as their former teacher. Though I could no longer wield the power of evaluation, I still sat in a position of authority, and the women may have felt some urge to please. This desire, prevalent in the culture even outside the research setting, is based on the belief that getting along with another person is more important than pushing one's viewpoint (Jones, *Values*). I would thus characterize the relationship between us as asymmetrical-trust, an unequal relationship between the interviewer and interviewee (Lincoln and Guba 269), but a relationship I sought to equalize with multiple interviews with the participants and their designated family member.

The most apparent bias in this study, as in many other qualitative studies, is my positionality as an outsider. Though my husband and I have lived in the region since 1975 and I would label myself an acculturated outsider, I am still aware of how misrepresented Appalachia has been and heed Stephen Hanna's caution that "no intimate insider or detached outsider can see all of the region or can create a representation that does not reference existing texts" (203). Saying that, I also believe that living in the area for thirty years and getting to know the people in daily interactions has given me the right to "make a knowledge claim" and create an "ethos acceptable to the Other" (Cintron 3), the women in this study.

In fact, my time spent in the region and my interactions with the women accounted for the ease with which I gained their trust as I initiated this research. An example of that trust occurred when I reviewed the informed consent form and asked the women to sign it. Each participant smiled at me as I went over the need for their protection as human subjects, as if to say, "I'll sign this form to make you happy, but we already have a relationship, and I trust you." Though I believe in participants' right to know about the full nature of the research project, how they will be involved, and their right to withdraw, I resonated with sociologist Murray Wax's concept of a covenant of trust. Unlike biomedical research where the subject needs protection, "the potential host community [of the qualitative researcher] does not typically require protection from the researcher; and, since neither party yet knows the consequences of the intrusion, 'informed consent' becomes a fantasy" (28). I built on the "covenant of trust" in our interviews.

Looking at other studies of qualitative research, I noted that Donehower's entry into her Appalachian community was easier because she was related to some of the townspeople, but, as she writes, "my education, my dialect, and the fact that I was research-ing a doctoral dissertation all served to distance me from those I interviewed" (*Beliefs* iii). Seitz highlighted the advantages of being an outsider in her study of Appalachian women in community organizations: "I was . . . not restricted by ties of kinship and place in an uncertain economic environment, and outside the commitments of collective associations" (19). Like Elizabeth Chiseri-Strater and Bonnie Sunstein, I tried to strike a balance of "an outsider 'stepping in' and an insider 'stepping out' of the culture [I] study" (6) in order to make the ordinary seem extraordinary (8). Though I was an outsider with longevity in the community, I had to admit that, like David Barton and Mary Hamilton, my "geographical origins and . . . educational background" were different from my adopted neighbors (xvii). Though I believe that outsiders can mirror strengths of a culture, I knew I would have to be careful of how I represented the Preston County women. Beyond the mirror that "only does one thing and shows us what we expect to see," I hoped that I could hold a window up to these women for them not only to see the reflections of their strengths but also to see out and to let the world see in; for "when they look at the outside world—what many academics would tout to them, they see that what they have is better" (Vanderbrake, e-mail).

Confronting my biases, I worked to involve the women in reading and revising their transcripts and in communicating with them after the interviews by letter and by phone, a measure that guarded against any misconceptions or misinterpretations and helped these women trust the whole process as they contributed to a new body of knowledge. I watched carefully to avoid slanting the research to favor the victim, smoothing over unpleasant details, or looking beyond the issue being researched (Kirsch and Mortensen; Newkirk). Interviewing their family members provided another way to interpret the data and to represent them ethically.

Collecting Data

Aware of the strength of the women in my classroom, I wanted to assume a research stance that magnified the voices of these women to a national audience. Wanting to "validate and improve women's lives, not simply observe and describe them" (Kirsch and Mortensen xxi), I chose naturalistic rather than quantitative methods to determine literacy practices since college. As a classroom teacher, I wanted to be able to actively observe, question, learn, and ultimately become a better teacher with knowledge gained from my former students (Bissex), even though the study was not classroom-based.

Knowing how interviews in particular are suited to women (Reinharz) and knowing how case studies can portray the uniqueness of the participants in a way that would not be possible in larger, quantitative studies (Neilsen; Purcell-Gates; Merrifield et al.; Barton and Hamilton), I decided that these techniques would be the most effective for my research.

Interviews

I scheduled interviews during January and February 1999. In my first phone calls, I recalled their impression on me personally and academically during the time I had taught them and how much I had wanted to tell their stories to those outside the region. For those who agreed to be part of the study, I began each interview by becoming reacquainted and reviewing the importance of the informed consent forms and other administrative matters. Then I began asking questions on reading and writing in their jobs, homes, and communities. I reviewed my plans to eventually choose three of them for in-depth case studies, which would include shadowing them on their jobs, interviewing family members about literacy's effect on the family, and interviewing them again with more questions to complete the research. The interviews generally lasted an hour or more and were guided by a list of questions.

Because the place of the interviews was crucial for communication purposes (Belenky et al.), I let these women pick the site. Four interviews took place in my office and four in their job settings. I traveled no more than a half hour to their places of work, which included two public schools, the local hospital, and a private counseling center. I found the two school settings difficult because of interruptions from co-workers, public address system announcements, and poor room acoustics. In spite of these factors, we managed to converse, and these women contributed a great deal to my research.

In the interviews, I defined the purposes of the study and of literacy as the use of symbol systems in our culture, which included traditionally understood reading and writing as well as literacy in context: grocery lists, recipes, catalogs, and so on. I divided the questions into three sections: pre-college, during college, and post-college. In the pre-college section, I asked what sort of reading and writing they did with their families, who or what influenced them to go to college, and whether they were the first in their families to attend. These questions gave me some ideas about their literacy background and their motivation for going to college.

The second section focused on reflections and evaluation of their college experiences in relation to managing academic discourse within the college and balancing college work with other obligations. I asked how they changed their home literacy habits to suit college demands; what changes they noted in themselves from freshman to senior year; what was most or least helpful in college; how being in college affected their families, their home life, and their children; and how they viewed the writing they did in my class. Their answers informed me about their lives within and without the college during that time.

The final section of questions focused on their post-college literacy practices in home, community, and work and sought information about achievement of the hopes and dreams expressed in class; their activities since graduation; their evaluation of how college prepared them for their jobs (if it did); what sort of reading and writing they did at home, in their communities, and on the job; whether their children who had graduated from high school had gone on to college or postsecondary education; and their evaluation of the total college experience (see appendixes A and C for lists of questions for participants).

In the initial interviews, I listened for information about literacy development for all eight women, but I had another ear listening for who among the eight would be the most effective case study participants. As I ended each session, I explained what the rest of the study would involve, then asked them to fill out an information sheet to indicate their availability for further interviews. Two of the eight checked that they would be unavailable. From the rest, I used the following criteria for choosing the final three participants:

- Time out of school since graduation (from four to six years). With this criteria, I could determine literacy uses based on work experience. A student too recently graduated would not have had those details to offer.
- School achievement (women who were minimal, average, and outstanding students). It would have been easy to choose the superior students who generally make a study look good. Choosing a broader representation of achievement could illustrate a connection (or none) between achievement inside and outside the classroom.
- Career achievement (women who are unemployed and employed). Though there were two women in the original eight who were underemployed, the case study participants represented the two main categories above. This category could connect workplace literacy and point out uses of literacy by unemployed persons.

After I carefully reviewed all eight interview transcripts, I sincerely wanted to do case studies on all eight women, but time was too limited. To decide on the three, I consulted my dissertation director, close friends, and colleagues. From the beginning, I wanted to choose Lucy because of her poignant story and Jean because of her spunk and insatiable desire for more education. I was unsure of the third person because of my interest in both Polly's and Sarah's stories. After numerous e-mails and phone conversations with my dissertation director and my co-researchers Tina and Connie, I chose Sarah. Calling each of the three to ask if they were interested in being part of the case study, I was happy when they agreed. The rest of the study included shadowing the three women on their jobs, interviewing a family member to determine broader effects of education, and scheduling a final interview with them to tie up loose ends.

Transcription Protocol

Recording and transcribing created many issues that I wanted to approach sensitively. I hired Tina to transcribe the interviews. After she completed each transcript, I replayed the tapes and verified data, clarifying any inaudible remarks and adding nonverbal information. Though she had gone to college at a traditional age, Tina shared observations about each woman and assisted me in the important decision of how to transcribe Appalachian English. She believed that most Appalachian women, especially college graduates, would be self-conscious about their dialect.

To help us decide about what to do regarding transcribing dialect, I consulted several sources. Wendy Bishop, writing about ethnography, suggests that "unless dialect or pronunciation or timing is an element being examined by the researcher, there is no reason not to default in an interview transcript to an informal, but lightly edited presentation of speech" (107). Deborah Brandt, commenting on editing her transcriptions into "standard written English," notes that "such editing indeed washes out the dialectal diversity of the people I spoke with. However, not trained as a linguist, I lacked the skill to transcribe accurately the range of regional accents and dialects that I heard" (*Literacy* 13). In another source, Appalachian ethnographer D. E. Walls defends his choice to regularize language by stating that the "attempt to use the vernacular misfires in one of two directions. Either it confuses and slows down the reader or it reduces the mountain characters to little more than ignorant, comic fools. I had no desire to do either" (xiii). Though all language systems are rule-governed and legitimate, I wanted my audience to hear these women as intelligent beings who had something to whistle and crow about; I did not want someone judging them as "ignorant, comic fools."

Accepting the advice of these authors, Tina and I decided to regularize all nonstandard verbs and to leave in idioms and colloquialisms. To preserve the dignity of these women, we changed some of their nonstandard language (*she doesn't* for *she don't; it wasn't anything* for *it wasn't nothing*). I did not violate the intention of their utterances and hopefully have represented them "in a dignified and appropriate . . . manner" (Bishop 143).

Participant Observation

Based on recommendations from my dissertation committee, I decided after the first interview that I would observe or shadow the case study participants on their jobs before I scheduled another interview. Observing these women in their work and home settings would allow me to "see the world as [my] subjects see it, to live in their time frames, to capture the phenomenon on its own terms, and to grasp the culture in its own natural, ongoing environment" (Lincoln and Guba 273). Proceeding this way, I was able to check out further any incomplete information gathered from the shadowing experience and affirm literacy practices that I had observed and of which they may not have been aware. For a portion of one day, I observed the participants: Lucy and her toddler in her home, Jean in the Medical Intensive Care Unit at our local hospital, and Sarah at the private counseling agency where she is a foster care specialist.

This observation rewarded me on many counts: I saw how hard these women worked to perform well on their jobs; I saw caring and empathy exhibited for clients they served; and I noticed the connection of accurate and dependable reading and writing to serving their clients adequately. In Lucy's home (she did not work outside the home), I observed how literacy assisted her in the challenge of raising her children and in making a meaningful life for herself. (See table 1 for time spent with participants.)

Family Interviews

My next plan was to interview at least one adult relative of each woman to ask what literacy development he or she had observed in the participant's life since college. I had many reasons to involve family members in the research. Appalachian families are close, and female relatives helped care for the young children of Lucy, Jean, and Sarah while they attended school. Also, their mothers had encouraged them to go to college, supporting Marcia Egan's observations

Table 1. Time Spent with Participants

	Length of first interview	Amount of time shadowing	Time with family member	Length of final interview
Lucy	1 hour	3 hours	0	1 hour
Jean	45 minutes	4 hours	40 minutes	45 minutes
Sarah	1 hour	3 hours	2.5 hours	45 minutes
Five other participants	5 hours	not applicable	not applicable	not applicable

of the crucial role that male and female relatives have, even if the relatives (females in particular) occupy traditional roles. Finally, relatives can establish "a multigenerational perspective of the data" (Taylor and Dorsey-Gaines 226). Their opinions would add another perspective to the question of literacy development.

Because I sensed in conversations with my informants that their family members were reticent to talk to me alone, I decided to provide them with a preliminary list of questions ahead of the interview. I also encouraged the participants to be there with their family members to alleviate the possible discomfort of meeting me alone. Questions included reactions to their relative returning to college, the changes they observed in that person, and their personal feelings about education for women (see appendix B). Two of the three participants' family members complied; Lucy's family member could not arrange her schedule to see me.

Methods of Analysis

During the project, I looked at emerging data, refining research questions in the process. Looking for patterns, making discoveries, and coding or labeling categories within the material, I used the constant comparative method and chunking to analyze my data. In pre-college literacy, factors that emerged related to family education, influence, uses of literacy, and size and personal/school uses of literacy. During college, codes related to personal change in reading, writing, and adjustment to college; support or nonsupport of family; reasons for postponing college; learning style; involvement with children; uses of technology; and personal perceptions of college. For post-college literacy, the codes reflected current employment status, spouse disability, church and community literacy, definition of region, job advancement and post-college advanced degrees, literacy of spouse and children, and changes in family. The most difficult portion of this step was sifting through data to focus on essentials of literacy practices since college.

Writing This Book

During the time of writing this book, I read Appalachian author Chris Offutt's *No More Heroes* and was impressed with his presentation of interviews with his German-born parents-in-law. Instead of a dry summary of "he said," "I said," Offutt wrote the interviews in narrative form. I decided then to weave quotations from Lucy, Jean, and Sarah into narratives that offered more than "Lucy said," "I think." I had further verification for using narratives from my former professor Gian Pagnucci in his *Living the Narrative Life: Stories as a Tool for Meaning Making*. He believes that the language of narratives is a "language that shakes our world up, rearranges it, and makes us pause and look again" (50). Weaving these women's stories with the narrative of my literacy creates a personal view of literacy that can help us to "make sense of our worlds" (3). I believe that I have represented them accurately and made the reading more cohesive and enjoyable.

Ultimately this methodology provided the data and led to the findings that fill these pages. The Preston County study should add the voices of these women to the conversation about literacy in all of its contexts, for academic literacy was a small though important part of their everyday literacies.

Portraits

Though I could choose only three for case studies, the Preston County women all contributed to the general findings of literacy practices in this study. They impressed me during our interviews with their choice to flourish in spite of inauspicious conditions that might have discouraged others. All eight women reflect in sharp relief the determination of Appalachian women to challenge the cultural roles that define them and to grow like mountain flowers and trees penetrating these three-million-year-old mountain ledges.

Judith

Born and raised in these mountains, Judith brought to mind maidenhair ferns that cover the moist ground of surrounding forests. Though graceful and delicate like the fern, she is tenacious. When her husband "slipped and fell down a steel stairway about seven feet" and could no longer work in the mines, Judith accepted the responsibility of being the primary breadwinner. She went into education to earn a salary that would provide for her husband and two girls still in school since her husband's disability payments were not enough. From a family of five where both parents graduated from high school, Judith recalled with fondness her memory of traveling as a toddler with her school-aged aunts to the nearby one-room school. After finishing high school, she entered college for a short time and dropped out when her husband moved to Texas for military service. Waiting approximately twenty years, Judith re-entered college and majored in middle grades education, graduating in December 1997. Though struggling in composition class, Judith reported that my encouragement motivated her to do well. When I asked her to describe the changes in herself from freshman to senior year, she replied:

> Well, I think college helped me mature a lot and see the real me. Before that, I had been mother, wife, all this and that. And this time I felt I was doing something for me personally. Even though it was for family, it was something that I really, you know, I'm doing this for myself . . . to please myself. (February 5, 1999)

Judith enjoyed college and believed that she was modeling education's importance for her daughters. Like the maidenhair fern spreading out over the forest bottom in spring, Judith spread her knowledge in her new job as a seventh grade math teacher, a job she secured eight months after graduation.

Hope

Another of my former students, Hope, reminded me of the redbud tree, whose blossoms announce spring, hope after the harsh winter months. Like the redbud trunk that gets stronger as it grows, Hope became strengthened by literacy models in her mother and then her stepmother after her mother's death. They taught her dad, who had gone only to second grade, how to read:

> If he [her dad] needed to know how to read something, she [her mother] taught him. That's how he learned how to write his name and everything. He couldn't pick up a newspaper and read it. But anything he had to read at work, he could read, but he couldn't read us stories or anything. (January 20, 1999)

Her mother encouraged both Hope and her sister to get an education to become teachers. As the redbud heralds spring, so her education degree became her new beginning, teaching special education on the elementary level with a solid basis of preparation from her Preston College education classes. Because jobs were not plentiful at the time she graduated, she had to take a job seventy minutes away from her home over narrow, winding roads, made longer if she trailed a coal truck traveling the same way. As redbud pods create new shoots spread by wind and birds, so Hope's teaching enabled special education students to be successful.

Mary

Along the roads these women travel are field daisies accessible to all who may stop, flowers that recalled the personality of another informant, Mary. Dark-haired and wide-faced, eyes alert to the world about her, Mary grew up in a family of six whose mother left high school her senior year and whose father completed third grade and later vocational school in welding and mechanics. Like daisies, Mary responded to life with openness typified by her decision to attend college fourteen years after dropping out in eighth grade:

> My sister [a high school junior] called me up and wanted me to take the ACT with her. . . . None of her friends were going that day, so she didn't want to go by herself. So she picked me up an information packet from the guidance counselor. And I filled it out and went with her—actually scored higher than she did. (February 2, 1999)

She thought, "Well, I've done this, so I just called the college and asked a few questions, and I applied and was accepted." Once in college, Mary grasped the writing process and did well, writing about the activities of her life. Her biggest concern in college was losing her common sense, something that had been modeled for her by her eighty-six-year-old grandmother.

Because of the poor job market for teachers, she was unable to find a teaching position upon graduation. To support her disabled husband and two sons, she did substitute teaching and took such jobs as a K-Mart photographer; at the time of the study, she was a data entry clerk for an environmental lab. After college, she extended her literacy to designing her own Web page on which she posted family photographs, her poetry, poetry links, and descriptions of her family, making herself more accessible, like the field daisies along the road.

Faith

Another Appalachian wildflower, the lady slipper, suggested the personality of Faith. Like a pink or yellow orchid that surprises the hiker in the woods with its splendor, hiding among the forest floor or on rock outcroppings, Faith is shy in a crowd, surprising the listener with her quiet intelligence and perfectly crafted work. The seventh in a family of nine, she reported that neither of her parents completed high school; her mother made it to eighth grade and her father to early elementary school. Both modeled reading, especially her dad, who educated himself by reading *National Geographic* and

Louis L'Amour westerns. Three of her brothers attended college, but she was the only girl in her family who attended. Faith's husband, who had three years of college and dropped out for financial reasons, worked as postmaster in a small town about twenty miles from Preston College, and at the time of the interviews, she had two children, one in junior high and one in high school.

Her main reason for returning to college was that, "after my oldest started to school, education seemed to be really important . . . you know, my going to college would be a kind of influence on him." Though an experienced reader and writer of stories when she was ten or eleven, she hated writing in high school, and so in freshman composition she "had to really work hard at writing. . . . It was hard for me to express what I wanted to say" (January 26, 1999). Though Faith valued her education, she was frustrated with the lack of teaching positions close to home, where she wanted to remain because of her two children still in school.

Polly

Another participant, Polly, reminded me of the wild azalea, a late spring flower with baseball-sized clusters of bright orange or pure white flowers growing under trees in moist ground. Like the flower, she radiates joy and confidence, especially regarding her college education; she stated how she would always be able to use what she learned in her life even if she never got a teaching degree. What motivated Polly to attend college was her divorce. She reflected:

> Well, what could I do? And, well, I talked to some people and stuff and somebody suggested to me, you know, "Why don't you try college?" And I thought, "No, I couldn't go to college because that's just for eighteen-year-olds. I couldn't go up there and be with them, you know." And they said, "No, there's a lot of older people up here, people your age." And I thought I would try it. (January 21, 1999)

Like Faith's parents, Polly's parents had finished eighth grade, but Polly had the distinction that none of the other participants had—seven of nine aunts and uncles had graduated from college; one was a NASA scientist. Waiting seventeen years between high school and college, Polly, who also majored in early elementary education, experienced some negative reaction: "They [her family] didn't think I was smart enough or that my grades would be good, or that I could even handle it with having a family, too."

After graduation, Polly spent years doing substitute teaching before she finally accepted the city clerk position in a nearby town, a job for which her college degree was an asset. She reflected on her love of reading and writing in our interview: "I don't know how people make it without reading and writing. I seriously don't. And I feel so sorry for them, because I KNOW the people." In addition to her city clerk work, she used literacy at home to read, to look up information, and to keep a journal, activities that kept the color in her life like the wild azalea.

Lucy

The first of the three case study informants, Lucy reminded me of a black-eyed Susan, a bright flower that beckons passersby from the highway in midsummer. Her jocular personality, in spite of spouse abuse and her child's health problems, mirrors the black-eyed Susan's ability to survive in all sorts of conditions. She grew up as the middle of five children and was, at the time of this study, a single mother of an eight-year-old son and a two-and-a-half-year-old daughter with cystic fibrosis.

Lucy pointed to terrible public school experiences, especially to what she called generational teachers, teachers whose mothers, fathers, aunts, and uncles had taught in that school for years. She went on to say:

> I have always been large, and our family with seven kids has always been poor, and the teachers had no use for me or my family. Though they never discouraged me, they had their little special kids to pay attention to. (February 4, 1999)

She illustrated the two-edged nature of literacy when she described the story of her abusive husband who would not allow her to carry schoolbooks into the house. For Lucy, attending college was an activity that energized her, and she "hated to leave at the end of the day because I had to face my husband, Matt."

Majoring in art and graduating in 1996 from Preston College, Lucy spent her time helping others in trouble and taking care of her children. Like the black-eyed Susan open to the world, Lucy wrote letters to the editor on subjects as varied as deadbeat dads, local school conditions, and other community concerns.

Jean

When I thought of Jean, I remembered our first meeting at 8 A.M. and marveled at how alert she was at the end of her twelve-hour shift, like sunshine opening up a morning glory. She spent time pursuing numerous building projects and other hands-on physical work in addition to her nursing job and continuing education courses. Jean's parents did not finish school—her mother made it to eighth grade and her dad to early elementary school. Like Mary, Jean dropped out of high school, though she made it to tenth grade, and decided to take the GED on a lark when her husband became disabled twenty years later. Surprised that she did so well, she thought she would enroll in the PC nursing program. Her weak academic skills made it necessary for her to take three and a half years to complete her two-year nursing degree, but like the morning glory climbing the fencepost, Jean was persistent enough to keep moving. She failed the proficiency exam at the end of the semester, which required her to repeat the class. She says:

> Coming back was just like starting school over again. But you can take anybody that's willing to learn and teach her anything, and if you take one twenty years later, and she knows nothing about a particular subject matter, if she wants to, she'll learn. It just takes the will to! (April 25, 1999)

With the seeds of academic success planted with her, Jean was amassing continuing education and other credits to enrich her life since her college experience, though she continued to view herself as a poor reader. She believed that she could make a difference in what she passed along to her children and grandchildren yet to be born: "I hope that my grandchildren will not, if I have anything to say about it, drop out of school as I did. And they will love reading more than I did." Jean can then watch her grandchildren bloom as she did with a college degree.

Sarah

Sarah, another participant, called to mind the spring beauty flower, which appears to be fragile but has tough roots and grows by itself or in clusters in the dark creek beds among the dead leaves of fall. Sarah is an attractive woman who prefers the solitary life because of the intensity of her work with severely abused children and her determination to raise her son with good morals and values. Though married when she came to college, Sarah's attainment of an education contributed to her eventual divorce two years after graduation, since her husband accused her of becoming too independent. Sarah shared with the other women a determination to succeed, though her academic background was different from either Lucy's or Jean's. Attending college seven years after high school, Sarah was an excellent student who had been heavily influenced by her mother, Naomi, to go to college, where Sarah graduated cum laude with a degree in psychology/human services. Reflecting on that day, Sarah said:

> I guess the one thing that made it [going to college] all seem worth it to me was on graduation day when my mom got to stand there and watch the dream come true. And just as soon as they started playing the music, my mom started crying. So that is what I worked hard for. Her dream and my dream. (January 25, 1999)

Sarah was employed as a foster care case manager in a private counseling agency and was working to get a master's degree in social work. Sarah emerged from a fatherless childhood to succeed academically in high school and college and to become a person who helped others in trouble.

These women did not come to the college voiceless, though the academic setting silenced them during their first years there. In the chapters that follow, these women's individual stories contribute to a chorus of whistlin' and crowin'. Table 2 provides a concise description of the eight women.

Table 2. Participant Descriptors

	Judith	Hope	Mary	Faith	Polly	Lucy	Jean	Sarah
Parents' education	mother and father, high school diploma	mother, high school diploma; father, 2nd grade	mother, left high school in 12th grade; father, 3rd grade and vocational school	mother, high school diploma; father, 8th grade	mother and father, 8th grade	mother, 8th grade; father, high school diploma and vocational school	mother, 8th grade; father, early elementary	mother, 8th grade; father, unknown
Family size	4	3	6	9	2	7	3	2
Marital status	married, spouse disabled	married, spouse laid off	married, spouse disabled	married, spouse working	divorced, remarried	divorced	married, spouse disabled	divorced
Children	2 married sons; 2 daughters in high school; 2 grandchildren	1 married son; 1 son in high school; 1 grandchild	1 grown son; 1 son in high school	1 son in high school; 1 daughter in junior high	1 daughter and 1 son married; 1 son in high school; 3 grandchildren	1 son, elementary school; 1 daughter, 2.5 years	1 grown son; 1 daughter married; 1 son in high school	1 son in high school
High school diploma	yes	yes	no	yes	yes	yes	no	yes
Years between high school and college	24	19	15	20	17	10	20	7
Degree and graduation date	middle grades education, Dec. 1997	early elementary education, May 1995	early elementary education, May 1993	early elementary education, Dec. 1993	early elementary education, May 1995	art, May 1996	nursing, May 1997	psychology, May 1993
Evaluation of college	enjoyed every minute; role model for daughters	prepared her well for special education teaching	gave her life skills that she has used in various jobs	prepared her for teaching	learned life skills; built up self-esteem	increased self-esteem; "getaway place" from abusive husband	turned her life around	raised self-confidence; a good foundation for her job

Table 2. Participant Descriptors (continued)

	Judith	Hope	Mary	Faith	Polly	Lucy	Jean	Sarah
Current job	7th grade math teacher	special education teacher, K–5th grade	data entry clerk for environmental lab	Title I assistant teacher	city clerk	homemaker; cares for child with cystic fibrosis at home	intensive care unit nurse	foster care worker
Unique traits	attended college after high school; dropped out to get married	mother urged, "Go to college and be a teacher."	took ACT on a lark; scored 21 on first try; applied to college	received associate of arts degree; waited 20 years to come back	7 of 9 aunts and uncles have college degrees; one is a NASA scientist	abusive spouse refused books in house; she did all studying at college	took and passed GED on a lark; applied to nursing program	father killed in mines when she was 5; mother wanted college for her

2 / Theory and Context
Silence, Voice, and Identity

> All [academic authors] have written about . . . the need to
> reclaim a memory, memory of an identity in formation and
> constant reformation, the need to reclaim a memory of an
> identity as formed through the generations.
> —Victor Villanueva, "Cuentos de mi Historia"

As I heard the stories of the Preston County women, I observed them move from silence in the academic classroom to a revised identity to a more confident voice in their communities. Reflecting on their stories, I began to see the parallels to my own search for voice, the need to "reclaim a memory of an identity." Slowly, I began to acknowledge that the "reasons we engage in academic endeavour are often connected . . . implicitly to our own experiences and desires . . . our own history and interests" (Lillis 2).

Looking back through a generation, I remembered my first voice, nurtured fifty some years ago in Greensboro, North Carolina, where I grew up as the oldest of eight, the daughter of Leo and Teresa Kelleher. My voice emerged among numerous silences: my mother's silence in a family of thirteen, which strengthened her resolve to raise eight children to know the value of work, education, and equality; my silence in a northern college, which strengthened my resolve to show that southern women are not idiots; my later silence as a long-term part-time college instructor, which strengthened my resolve to return for doctoral work; my silence in the doctoral classroom born of fear of failure; and other silences in between. In fact, I observed how our mutual coming to voice fit the three different meanings of voice reflected in Elisabeth Hayes's essay "Voice" in her co-edited book with Daniele D. Flannery, *Women as Learners: The Significance of Gender in Adult Learning:* voice as language, identity, and power.

Voices

Voice as Language

> You can't be a voice box for your own feelings and experiences, much less for those of your place, if you've accepted that your first speech was wrong. For if you abandon or ridicule your voiceplace, you forfeit a deep spiritual connection. . . . It is nurture, humor, memory, vision. It is what we must get back to in order to know ourselves, the "first voice" that teaches us to speak.
>
> —Georgia Ella Lyon, "Voiceplace"

Lyon speaks eloquently about the importance of reclaiming "first voice," the regional dialect that has been the object of ridicule and a clear distinction of class and social and cultural identity. In what follows, I reflect on the connection of voice and language, using Hayes's definition of voice as talk, which she states can "signify women's actual speech or speaking style . . . focus[ing] on how women use spoken language in learning situations and how their learning preferences may be reflected in their use of talk" ("Voice" 80). This section concentrates on the first part of the definition, the actual speaking style or dialect of the women and me.

Though I did not grow up with missionaries or government workers telling me I was culturally deprived like the Preston County women and Appalachians in general did, I did get the message from insiders as well as outsiders that my first voice was not Proper. All of the teachers in our Catholic schools were nuns from Maryland and Philadelphia who came south to "mission" territory. Mother herself corrected our grammar constantly, so we got the message that if we didn't speak well and become educated, we would not do well. The summer before I went off to St. Joseph's College in western Maryland, Mother sent me to Mrs. Ainsworth's two-week charm school to learn social etiquette, which included diction lessons, so that I would not embarrass her while I was at school. Once I was there, my speech teacher with a broadcasting degree from the University of Maryland spent hours with me outside the classroom, trying to cleanse my speech of its regional quality. People would ask me to talk for them as they broke into peals of laughter. Well-meaning people said, "You're pretty smart for a southerner." My first voice was shadowed by many others saying it wasn't good enough; therefore, I changed my dialect and accumulated college degrees to define myself as better, as smarter. I mastered Standard English, and people stopped to listen without laughing.

When I came to eastern Kentucky, I had a hard time understanding the dialect and accent, especially when I traveled out into Preston County. When I began teaching, students thought I was from Boston, not North Carolina. Before my recent doctoral work, I thought of their speaking as poor grammar; there I learned about Appalachian English, "a highly stigmatized variety of American English" (Puckett, *Seldom* xiii). Though speakers in the region do not limit themselves to speaking one way and frequently intermingle standard and nonstandard language (Hymes), and though "no dialect can be seen as inferior or superior to another" (Edwards and Giles; Labov; Trudgill; Milroy and Milroy), the social judgment about Appalachian dialect and other nonstandard varieties keeps people in the region subordinate, economically unequal, and less respectable, illustrating that "racial discrimination and internalized racism are often inseparable from intolerant attitudes toward different languages and dialect" (Okawa 111).

Numerous studies illustrate the prejudices of school-educated people toward nonstandard speakers, the most pertinent being Reid Luhman's matched guise study, "a technique [that] involves asking interviewees to evaluate the personal qualities of speakers whose voices are recorded on tape, whereby *the same* speaker uses *different* linguistic varieties" (Obiols). In this study of eastern Kentucky speakers at a Kentucky state university, speakers of Appalachian English were judged as lacking ambition, intelligence, and education, though their grades proved otherwise. He also found that standard speakers are more respected than loved, that respondents felt more solidarity with speakers of lower status and less solidarity with speakers of higher status, and that book learning cancels common sense (Luhman).

Since language marks economic class and "since it is not so easily shed as a suit of clothes or a rusted and aging automobile . . .

[language] symbolizes our social experience in an intimate way and locates us within significant social groups from which we draw our identities" (Luhman 332). In her research of an Appalachian community in western North Carolina, Kimberley Donehower observed that participants recognized and spoke Standard English, but they wanted "those around them to acknowledge . . . that [standard English is] not the only way to talk and write" (*Beliefs* 199). She goes on to say:

> Informants generally knew that their dialect was one of the primary markers of their identity as Southern Appalachians, and this man [a school principal] was quick to defend their right to speak it: "our dialect, the mountain dialect, is just a—an area dialect, and that's just the way the, the speech you know. A lot of, a lot of the mountaineers still use 'holped' for 'helped.' And, and you'll hear this, but it's what, you know, it's just something that's instilled in them, it's not—it's correct English *for them*. And our English and our dialect is just as correct for us around here as any in Chicago, or New York, or you go to Canada, you'll have a little blend of the French, in it. (*Beliefs* 98–99)

In my experience of living and teaching in the region, I have found that students can complete four years of college and still sound as if they came from "the head of the holler," a phrase used by local people to designate those who are isolated, don't get out much, and hence speak with a heavy accent. The students in my classroom worry about losing their family connections if they "get above their raisings" by speaking in what they call a "citified" speech. They also, like the school principal above, want respect for their native tongue.

Sensitivity about dialect comes from these internalized attitudes from outsiders. As described in chapter 1, I sought to deflect attention away from these women's exact language patterns and settled on a lightly edited version of their speech. It was therefore surprising that when I asked the participants to review their interview transcripts,

Jean, one of the case study informants, edited her transcript even further, saying that she did not want to sound like a "hillbilly" to anyone else reading the transcript.

Though there was no specific question about dialect listed for all participants, I did ask the case study participants if their teachers had attempted to correct their speech. Lucy said that the teachers had sounded like her and that any discrimination had been based on her being poor and obese. Jean stated that teachers had not motivated her as a practical learner, so she had lost interest, but reported no pressure to speak differently. Similarly, Donehower's school principal responded that none of his teachers had asked him to change his dialect.

However, when they came to Preston College, they experienced some disjuncture with faculty attitudes toward Appalachian dialect. The message they got was that their dialect was not acceptable in academic writing or in speech classes or in future job interviews. A colleague in a nearby college states that her school's teacher education faculty have worked with students on voice and diction to little avail, because once the students become classroom teachers, they return to their old ways (Vanderbrake, personal interview). Min-Zhan Lu, in a recent *CCC* article, states that compositionists need to combat the divisions of the world based on standard and non-standard uses of English. She would rejoice at the resistance of these women to serve their own interests, to adapt Standard English to their own uses rather than to buy into the gospel of the "most Literate of the most Developed" country (46).

Linguist Michael Montgomery in his work on Appalachian English points to the diversity of the language and would concur with sociologist Paula Moore that trying to make language more homogeneous is like taking the color out of a painting (qtd. in Caudill and Quillen). Linda Scott DeRosier states that the language is "colorful, earthy, profane, and . . . a very important part of our identity as hill folk, and . . . not something we should give up without a fight" (58). By maintaining their first voice, the Preston County women have learned the power of language that they use in their communities in positive ways. Kentucky-born DeRosier states that she is at home in both communities (academic position as professor at the University of Montana and daughter of a Kentucky coal miner) because she makes an effort to watch her language in both settings, thereby not offending her relatives. She says:

> My sense of who I am comes from my identity as a hillbilly woman, and I do not see that ever changing. . . . To maintain a sense of wholeness and of loyalty to the community that I was brought up in, I have held on to an accent that is too often mistakenly seen as an indication of lower intelligence than many other accents in the US. (66–67)

Language is closely tied to the way women define themselves and create community, and changing that language is a method of erasing culture.

Voice as Identity

> If I hadn't come to college, I wouldn't be the person I am now. I wouldn't trade that growth or the knowledge I've gained. Yeah, I'm glad I did that. I'm glad I did that. It made me a better person.
>
> —Mary (February 2, 1999)

Though she had not been employed in the teaching field since college and was underemployed in her present job, Mary reflected positively on the college's contribution to her identity during our interview. Her response echoes the awareness I came to when I finished the course work for my doctorate. Like the Scarecrow in *The Wizard of Oz* who wanted a brain and finds out from the Wizard that "you've had a brain all along!" so the experience with my doctoral work reinforced my intellect in a way that no other experience could have. This common experience of being smart but not knowing it is reflected in other literacy studies about women, most notably those of Jennifer Horsman and Wendy Luttrell.

Generally, the Preston County women like Mary had not been voiceless in the context of their families; they had strong identities as mothers, wives, and daughters but felt "inarticulate when [they] enter[ed] a college classroom" (Hayes, "Voice" 94). Voice in this sense "focuses on how women's identity is reflected in what they say, in the ideas they express, and in the confidence they express in their own thoughts and opinions" (80). I would add that this confidence emanates into all aspects of their lives, far beyond the personal, to families, spouses, and children as well as to community acquaintances.

Going to college assisted the women in the Preston County study to become somebody, to make their voices heard. Like them, I turned the silence of fifteen years as an adjunct to action by enrolling at the age of fifty in the Indiana University of Pennsylvania doctoral program, a step toward identity, toward the need to be seen, to be recognized as having authority, so that I would be hired full-time and be recognized as a professional by colleagues and students. My identity as a nontraditional student prompted me to have a new respect for former nontraditional female students in my classroom and to see the possibilities of educating others about our stories.

One of the tools that academic literacy provided for the women in this study to help them achieve comfort in the academic setting was their writing in college. They reported some personal writing before college but spoke unkindly about school-sponsored literacy. Mary reflected a common theme in the interviews, students' struggle with college writing:

> At first I thought it [writing] would be difficult, but once I started learning some patterns about writing, how to get across what I wanted to, because you can't just write something down on paper, [it was not so hard]. There are certain steps you've got to take. And I was never taught those steps. (February 2, 1999)

These reflections surprised me since the women's writing was generally more lucid and creative than some of the traditional students. Their maturity and life experience made content easy to retrieve, and once they grasped the form, they illustrated writing's potential for working-class women to give words to their life expe-

riences, which in turn affirmed the power of the experience and of
their worthiness. They wrote about homemaking (the process of
making chocolate gravy or an eleven-layer apple stack cake) and
other issues important to women (the horrors of child and spouse
abuse and date rape, issues that cut across class boundaries). I believe that literacy, both reading and writing, offered these women
"the greatest force for empowering, validating, and affirming [them-
selves] and [their] self-worth" (Harrienger 151). In fact, many of
their essays ended up in the English department's publication of
teacher-nominated student essays, *Voices from the Hill* (see appendixes D, E, and F for case study essays).

Though speaking about traditional students' forming identity,
Robert E. Brooke considers identity formation in the writing classroom. While these women have constructed their social identity
beyond that of any traditional student, they still "position themselves to form an identity for the self." The women connect "the role
of self as writer with other roles in the culture outside the classroom
. . . [and] as someone who uses writing to further personal thinking and to help solve public problems" (*Writing* 5). Because they
generally have more roles to play—particularly those of spouse,
mother, sibling, and worker—than traditional students do, they may
make connections more quickly and write more "meaningfully" (5).

Though they had not written expository essays before, the
women reported writing poems, journals, and letters, forms of ex-
pression that Anita Puckett confirms are considered acceptable for
mountain women to do. In her literacy study in eastern Kentucky,
she reveals that "literate practices are God-given attributes of
women's 'nature' . . . provid[ing] contexts in which a woman can
negotiate her social, religious, and cultural identity" ("Let" 137).
Though women can acquire literacy, they are bound by cultural roles
not to get above their raisings; after all, as mentioned earlier,
"whistlin' women and crowin' hens, always come to no good ends."
Puckett observes that these women

> walk a literate tightrope, called upon to assert an identity that
> affirms "good" reading and writing skills but constrained by

cultural norms and social practices in the directions and
forms their writing can successfully assume to maintain
social propriety and their family name. ("Let" 143)

The Preston County women appear to have managed walking the
tightrope. Their stories show individual confidence in their master-
ing of the written code as steps toward identity within the academic
community. Recognizing the power of the written word, they became more active in expressing themselves, using writing to create
meaning and to contribute to their identity and move from discomfort with academic literacy to fulfillment.

Voice as Power

Whether I ever use it [education degree] towards teaching, I
will always use it in life.

—Polly (January 21, 1999)

Forming an identity and recognizing their self-worth, these women
came to power, though not in the sense of Hayes's definition that
"emphasizes women's development of a collective identity and oppression as women, and of the means to challenge this oppression"
("Voice" 80). In contrast to collective identity, the Preston County
women experienced power in their personal achievements, primarily by maintaining the closeness of their families. I believe with
Mary Field Belenky, Lynne A. Bond, and Jacqueline S. Weinstock
that as women are educated and are "drawn out and empowered,
they are likely to draw out and uplift others, who in turn will reach
out to still others. . . . Such women are more likely to be deeply
invested in seeing that the community meets the needs of all children and families" (7, 10). Their choice of work, their desire for
more education, and their influence on others make powerful statements, though they might not organize as a group. They prove that
"even those environments that may not seem optimal have given
women opportunities to create new knowledge, question old beliefs,
and engage in personal and social change" (Hayes, "Social" 52). Even
Lucy, who does not work outside the home and has not pursued an

education beyond college, has power in her local expertise role and in her frequent letters to the editor.

Even previous silences can empower women, as my mother, Teresa Kelleher, illustrated by numerous activities in her life. A frustrated intellectual who felt inferior because she had attended only one year of business college, Mother spent a lifetime instilling in her children, especially her daughters, the importance of literacy and education. Steeped in Catholic teachings about having large families and married to Leo Kelleher, who inherited his dad's scrap iron and metal business and whose salary was stretched by this family of eight, Mother thought education could help us achieve her dreams.

Enrolling us in the Catholic high school, which was integrated before the public schools were, Mother hoped we would get a good education and was alarmed at the exclusiveness of an invitation-only social club for the wealthy girls at our high school. With the ammunition provided by weeks of research on the damages social clubs can inflict on teens, Mother single-handedly and successfully challenged the school board to abolish the club that discriminated against blacks and working-class girls. Though it was difficult for my parents, they welcomed our new African American friends into our all-white, middle-class neighborhood home. Always a little bit irreverent, Mother and Dad challenged the bishop who forbade dances on our Catholic high school property because he feared interracial dancing and potential violence; they instead sponsored an integrated dance at a local Greensboro hotel for our senior class. When pickets formed to protest atrocities in Vietnam and El Salvador or Republican presidential policies that antagonized the poor, Mother was there. During the feminist movement, she took advantage of university courses offered for women returning to school, though she strongly objected to Betty Friedan and others excluding the voices of women like her own who chose to stay at home.

Turning voice into power, I completed my doctorate, an action that, next to marrying my husband and birthing my daughter and son, was the most joyful act of my life, followed only by receiving notification of the CCCC 2001 James Berlin Outstanding Dissertation of the Year Award. Mother's influence lives on in my daughter's work with female Appalachian folk artists and her position as fund-raiser for Appalshop, a socially activist Appalachian film media organization. Like his grandmother, my son marches in anti-war protests and fights for environmental causes. Power begets power.

The participants in this study, once they experienced the power of literacy and successfully learned about managing multiple tasks, became invested in the concept of lifelong learning, seeking advanced degrees in correspondence and satellite programs. Completing college, they knew that they were able to accomplish what they set out to do. Like other college graduates, these women

> learn much more than subject matter or skills. They learn implicit and explicit lessons about themselves as women and . . . about themselves as women of a particular race, class, and culture. These lessons in turn affect how they see themselves as learners and shape their future learning experiences. (Hayes, "Voice" 51)

Not content to remain in one position for too long, most of the employed women talked about job advancement. Mary, working in the lab at the time of this research, wanted to get a degree in English and work toward a master's, "and maybe someday, I'll get to teach on the college level" (February 2, 1999). Hope was planning in the summer of 1999 to go back for her master's, either in special education or in teaching reading on the elementary level, education that would help her move up the salary scale in the Preston County schools. When Judith finished her internship, she was planning to pursue graduate school. Jean's plans included getting numerous nursing certifications and working toward her master's in critical care nursing through correspondence. Sarah was aiming for a master's in social work. Lucy, working at home, was becoming more active in her son's school governance and continued to help others in various ways. All illustrate that literacy is social practice that

> demonstrates the changing demands that people experience at different stages of their lives and offers convincing

evidence of the need for lifelong learning systems which people can access at critical points when they need to re- spond to new demands. (Barton and Hamilton 282)

The women in this study gained economic power by making higher salaries without moving outside the community. Jean de- scribed the lack of economic power for women without college:

> I think it's a lot different for the girls than it is the boys. The boys can always get out and make a living. They can do something somewhere, somehow. Driving a coal truck, driving something, even though it's not what you want them to do, they can still make the money. But for a girl it's very hard. They can't get out and do what they want. And who wants to house clean for $5 an hour the rest of your life? It's fine; I've done it before. It's good. But you don't want to stay there the rest of your life. (April 29, 1999)

Without an education, residents in rural regions like Appalachia are harder hit by the dwindling economy, so job opportunities are lim- ited for men as well as for women. Not being aware of this, some may ask whether women entering traditional occupations don't just rein- force traditional low-paying work by keeping women in their places. The study participants chose traditional professions because there was no alternative. They moved from minimum wage jobs like retail and housekeeping, the only choices that Jean describes for women, to salaried positions as teachers, nurses, and social workers.

The power of literacy relates to the sense of accomplishment in finishing the college degree, something the women praised whether they found jobs in their majors or not. Their power rested in their awareness of being role models for their children, for the chance to be "somebody" (Luttrell), and for moving "from a pas- sive to an active role . . . to see themselves as . . . instrument[s] of knowledge and influence" (Neilsen 132). Like the African Ameri- can women in rural Georgia of S. Hammons-Bryner's study, the Preston County women's stories are those of "women who grow up in rural poverty, are poorly educated in classrooms where they suffer from denigrating remarks about their success potential, yet who dream, do more than wish, become change agents, and fulfill goals" (Hammons-Bryner 12).

Those who did not get jobs in their majors were frustrated with the job market, with perceived age discrimination, and with not being able to use talents they discovered during their four years at the college, and they blamed family pressures, the job market, and employers as opposed to blaming the college. Though we tend to hope that education enlarges women's vistas to consider nontraditional occupations, these Appalachian women did not have that many choices but achieved personal and social change, which they surely would not have been able to do otherwise. In other words, "Education does offer women opportunities, and the credentialist tie between education and work is as strong for women as it is for men" (Pascall and Cox 141). The key difference between their poor pre-college experience and college appeared to be that the women were "instrumental in shaping . . . their destiny" (Fiene 53).

One of the most powerful statements these women made was in their decision to remain in their communities: their acquisition of academic literacy did not destroy family or community. Though many are not opposed to moving away and becoming more upwardly mobile, the women knew how disruptive such a move would be for their families. So they overcame the objections some family members had to their returning to school and the constraints of gender roles and advanced beyond minimum wage jobs to get a college education, voicing their concerns by using literacy for their own purposes in their jobs, churches, children's schools, and homes, maintaining community values. These mountain women appear to be similar to Donehower's informants who

> use literacy within this system in the ways that they can, or to choose to opt out of this system as it operates in mainstream society by staying in their own communities, and enjoying a different kind of relationship with literacy as a result. (*Beliefs* 199)

This finding challenges previous literature about other non-mainstream groups who are alienated from their cultural moorings because of acquired academic literacy (R. Rodriguez; Bizzell; Dews and Law; Linkon; Shor; and others). Essays of working-class academics in *This Fine Place So Far from Home* illustrate that the academy "*has* destroyed something even while it has been re-creating [us] in its own image" (Law 1). For many immigrant groups, education creates "the clash and dislocation in our communities" (Rose 226), most notably depicted by Richard Rodriguez as he describes his estrangement from his home and native tongue, Spanish, as a result of his education. Though language change is an issue for these Appalachian women, it is not nearly as dramatic as it is for nonnative speakers of English, as exemplified in case studies of Appalachian and Californian nonliterates. Juliet Merrifield and her colleagues found that there was less concern "about the impact of literacy, language, and education on family relationships for the Appalachian group than for the California immigrants, some of whom fear the loss of their culture in following generations" (201). While educated Appalachians may leave the region for work, they usually come home often for visits, and so there is less risk of changing cultures. Likewise, there are many academics who manage to bridge the gap and not feel alienated.

The women in the Preston County study might have more economic power if they moved away, which in fact some Appalachians do. However, a colleague who formerly lived in Preston with her professor husband and was a nontraditional student in the Preston College English program pointed out to me the evolution of her thinking about people preferring to remain in the region:

> The magnificent, awe-inspiring beauty of Kentucky's hills and "hollers" and the sense of familial commitment made me see "wealth" and "resources" differently. Having been ping-ponged as academic gypsies, back-and-forth these past many years and realizing too late the negative impact that has on family, I know that "poverty" of soul and poverty of social ties are much worse than poverty of "stuff." (Knudson)

Though I do not mean to valorize poverty, Candy Knudson's awareness points to the value of remaining in the mountains rather than
uprooting entire families for the sake of upward mobility. In fact,
findings of a study of the alumni of twenty-three of the thirty-three
colleges that make up the Appalachian College Association reveal
that many graduates of its colleges of any age remain in the area,
supporting my findings (Pascarella et al.).

By taking their academic literacy and fitting it to their own
purposes, these women maintained the power of the common sense
and cultural integrity that they and other working-class students
feared they might lose by going to college (Soliday). One of the
participants, Mary, reflected in her interview on her eighty-six-year-
old grandmother, "I would give anything for her wisdom" (February 2, 1999). I found this same longing expressed in other readings.
Common sense, which the women feared losing, is defined as "the
commonly held conceptions of the world held by various cultures,
a culture's way of seeing and believing . . . carried and transmitted
by discourse" (Villanueva, *Bootstraps* 124). Resisting that loss and
not wanting to alienate themselves from their families, many may
drop out of college. In fact, common sense equates to personal
empathy and experience, which, for Horsman's adult education students, counted for more than an educated person's knowledge; in
other words, book learning does not equal "real" knowledge.
Luttrell's participants in her adult education classes in North Carolina and Philadelphia "were drawn to common sense and intuition
because these forms of knowledge rest in women themselves (not
in higher authorities) and are experienced directly in the world (not
through abstractions)" (32). Common sense, in reality, is a literacy
of its own with its own language and rules (Vanderbrake, personal
interview), though it generally stands in contrast to education, a
dichotomy that may not be so separate as the women feared (not
all educated people lack common sense).

The most important achievement of these nontraditional
women, an outgrowth of "the personal is political" argument, seems
to be "the sense of self-respect and worth gained from taking that
first step into college and sticking it out until they finish" (Shiber

2). Not getting work in their fields did not seem to matter as crucially as having something they did not have before. The narrative of the women in this study illustrates that "some people use literacy to make their lives more meaningful, no matter what their economic and political circumstances are" (Daniell, "Narratives" 404).

Summary

Recently, Mary called to see if I could help her find a publisher for her poems. In the middle of the conversation, she described the hours she had spent constructing her Web page and went on to say, "After the interview with you [in winter of 1999], I realized how much I missed writing, so I began writing poetry again." In addition to the poems, she had written several articles for a local newspaper, which were summaries of interviews with local bluegrass artists performing in the region. She informed me that she had quit her position as an environmental lab assistant to return to substitute teaching because the laboratory job, which she had at the time of the interviews, was just not satisfying her. Continually frustrated that she could not get a teaching job, Mary told me that the school principals she worked for were pleased with her work, but "when a job opens, somebody's cousin gets the job!" She has since moved to Pennsylvania, where she is teaching four-year-olds.

Because Preston is so small, I run into the eight women occasionally or talk to them on the phone as I did with Mary. At least quarterly, I see letters to the editor about her son's school conditions and related topics from Lucy (see appendix G), who has recently been elected to the Site Based Council at her son and daughter's school. She exhibited two works of art, a pencil drawing entitled *God, Naked in Our Sins* and a piece done in acrylics, *Memories,* in a recent alumni art exhibit at Preston College. Sarah called recently to tell me that she has taken a new job doing social work in a nearby county after quitting her job as director of a private social work agency. Hope finally found a teaching position closer to home than the two-hour round-trip commute to her other school. These and other conversations I have with these women confirm for me the continuing importance of literacy in their lives.

Maintaining their first voice, expanding their identity, and exercising personal power, these Appalachian women and I moved from silence to identity to voice. Below, I discuss the community in which they utilize their literacy, describing, among other things, the economic, educational, religious, and geographical aspects of their lives. How that context shaped these students and how it differs from mainstream culture might provide a new understanding of the tremendous odds they overcame to go to college and come to voice.

The Place of Appalachia

Prologue

As we wound our way through serpentine mountain roads behind dark behemoth coal trucks, I was silent with fear. It was September 19, 1975. My husband of one and a half years and I had left flat Baltimore city streets, traveled Interstate 81 through the Shenandoah Valley, and maneuvered West Virginia two-lane mountain roads before we reached the Kentucky state line. The mountains closed in around us as we traveled Route 119 in our army-green 1967 Dodge Charger filled with houseplants and suitcases. Only two weeks earlier we had come to Preston, a dark, claustrophobic town blackened with coal dust, for the interview at Preston College, located in the central Appalachian Mountains. After Mark was hired as dean of students, we sold our house, packed, and moved, thankful that one of us had a job.

Once we were settled in our two-story red brick home located in the center of campus on the hill above town, I thought we might have a visit from other college people, but no one came. Mark worked, and I pondered the superior résumé I had developed in Baltimore and waited until he came home to notice how clean the kitchen floor was. This move was more difficult than the one I made working for the Peace Corps in India about ten years earlier: I felt desolate and isolated, hemmed in by the mountains, far away from my friends and family.

Finally, I tired of worrying about how clean the house was and began interviewing for information, a technique I learned from a

Washington, D.C., headhunter for finding good jobs and one I thought might help me learn more about my new neighbors. With the help of college and church contacts, I identified community leaders to interview in the town and county; each of them recommended others to talk to, so eventually I spoke to about thirty people. Among that group were impressive women in positions of postmaster, county clerk, family planning director, and public health director. At different club meetings I was invited to attend, I began to listen to and observe the women in this region. A year later, when I became the director of continuing education, a program for which I successfully procured funding, I began to encounter other women who taught me more about the region. When I noticed the strength of mountain women instead of how unlike my circle of friends they were, I began to feel more at home. Having heard my mother preach constantly how every woman should be recognized for what she contributes to society no matter her position, I started to add all of this information together. Slowly, my attitude of superiority became dislodged, and my mainstream view of feminists as middle- or upper-class women fighting for jobs in order to break glass ceilings broadened.

If Mark and I were not convinced yet that Preston was our home, the welcome that our children, Laura and Brian, born two and four years later, received from the time people knew I was pregnant cinched our decision to stay beyond the five years we had originally planned.

As I look back on the thirteen-hour road trip we made that September of 1975 from Baltimore to Preston, I realize how significant our move was, and now I understand my fear. Moving from Maryland by the Atlantic to the steep and narrow valleys of the Appalachian Mountains, from a circle of our friends and college colleagues who were like family to a region where families were close and sometimes insular, from a familiar urban setting to a culturally different rural setting, we made an incredible leap. Now, having lived in the region for more than a quarter of a century, I understand that the lack of friendliness upon our arrival related to people waiting and watching to see if we liked it here, if we were going to keep ourselves on the mountain where the college is located, if we were going to "help" them like some missionaries had done, or if we were going to tell them how unhappy we were without the amenities of Baltimore. A hundred years of outsiders coming to the region preceded our arrival, outsiders who had used up resources and moved away or, like missionaries and government workers, had given the impression that local people could not solve their own problems and that their ways were somehow not good enough. Having been a Peace Corps volunteer, I know that the intentions of those programs might be good, but there is the danger of cultural imperialism, which demeans a region and silences the voices of its citizens.

The people to whom I had felt superior when we moved here continue to teach me about the values of independence, family, neighborliness, spirituality, and love. After they saw that we adopted Appalachia as our home, the people of the region, especially the women, embraced us so solidly that we eventually felt this place was more like home than the towns in Oregon and North Carolina where we were raised. When we return from out-of-town travels, we do not make the journey in fear as we did that first trip but with hope of coming home to the shelter and embrace of the people of these ancient mountains.

The description of the region that follows provides snapshots of our adopted home in my words, the words of the women, and the words of Appalachian scholars; it is not meant to be generalized to all Appalachians. Though we have lived in the region since that September day in 1975 and I have adopted the region as my home, I will always be an outsider and will have to pay attention to how problematic that is. Below I explore the context of Appalachia—the economy, education, religion, land, mountain values, and other realities—by contrasting it to Baltimore and other areas like it. I hope to describe "the stage on which the [women in this study] act out their lives" (Neilsen 2), situating the women's journey to college and beyond as they achieved voice in their communities.

The Economy

Perhaps the biggest contrast between Baltimore and Preston was the multiple economic resources in Baltimore and the one-industry extraction economy of Preston and the surrounding region. Having lived close to the Baltimore harbor, where we saw imported cars being unloaded and Bethlehem Steel spewing out factory workers at closing time, I moved to a region where I saw black-faced coal miners on their way home from work buying groceries. We got the chance to crawl in an underground mine to see what kind of work this coal mining was, and I learned that everything in Preston revolved around the industry. In addition to underground mining, I learned about surface mining, where coal seams were mined in the mountains. In either form of mining, miners loaded coal into coal trucks, which transported it to coal tipples, where it was loaded into railroad cars, which took the coal to electric plants. One such tipple sat at the bottom of the ninety-nine steps from the town to the college, and if we were trying to drive down from our campus house into town, we were often blocked and had time to count as many as 144 railcars waiting to be loaded and sent on their way. If we were really in a hurry, we parked and walked through the space between railroad cars, hoping they would not move. This condition changed when the tracks (and river) were rerouted during a massive mountain cut project.

Other regional employers outside of coal and coal-related businesses were small retailers, the hospital, and the county board of education. All were dependent on the fluctuation of a boom or bust economy, which offered numerous jobs during the boom but which accounted for job insecurity, leading to people leaving the region for work or living in poverty during times of bust. When we arrived in 1975, Preston County was in the middle of a boom, producing the most bituminous coal in the nation and featured in *National Geographic* in a story about the highest per capita millionaires, coal operators. During that boom, the county's population increased 33 percent (Rennick).

When I asked the women in this study about coal, they told me that jobs in the mines had supported their families: their fathers worked jobs like mechanic, electrician, and railroad worker. One of the participants' fathers moved to Michigan to work in the steel mills because of the fluctuating coal market. Mothers of the women

worked primarily as homemakers but took odd jobs such as hospital dietitian, school bus driver, small grocery store owner, aide in a
federal program, and house cleaner to provide basic needs for their
children. With the uncertainty of the job market, times were rough
growing up, especially in large families.

The women themselves married men who worked in the mines
with the exception of Faith, whose husband was postmaster in their
small town, and Polly, whose husband was a sanitation worker. One
of the main reasons cited by four of the eight women for going to
college was that their husbands had become disabled in or laid off
by the mines. Judith's husband became injured by falling down a
stairway in the mines and hurting his back, Jean's and Mary's husbands developed black lung disease, and Hope's husband was laid
off. Like the coal miners' wives in Carol A. B. Giesen's study, the
Preston County women lived daily with the threat of "death . . .
strikes, layoffs, and the seemingly inevitable black lung" (2). Those
who were married took on the traditional female role to take the
worry out of their husbands' lives, and they only occasionally
worked outside the home, like their mothers, in minimum wage jobs
since there were not many other choices. If they worked in low-
paying jobs, the women did not necessarily see it as "gender oppression but primarily as a result of economic conditions that have negatively impacted the working-class" (Ferretti 78).

Once the women were without their husbands' income or were
divorced, attending college and becoming academically literate was
the only way that they could get the skills to make a decent living.
At the time of this research, their college degree had given them
economic clout, which gave them more self-confidence and self-
esteem. Though not upwardly mobile in the traditional sense, they
moved upward from their previous incomes and added to the economic growth of Preston County, which Sarah describes as

> commercially growing. We've got super centers now even
> though I don't like them. We're supposed to get a civic cen-
> ter. We're slowly progressing, but we're not as far [along]
> as the big cities. I don't want us to ever be like the BIG

cities. But maybe a medium-sized one would be nice. (May 3, 1999)

Education

Unlike those who grew up in Baltimore who had their choice of public or private schools, depending on their neighborhoods or incomes, the Preston County women had no choice but to attend Kentucky schools in a system that was constantly rated at the bottom of the fifty states in terms of academic test performance. In fact, state and national literacy programs tout increased literacy in the Appalachian region as the solution to all of the area's economic problems, though scholars know the solutions are more complicated than the campaigns suggest. As Donehower states when people react negatively to her revelation that she is from Appalachia and has done research on the region, "The stereotype of Appalachian illiteracy is alive, well, and socially acceptable, and has been now for 120 years" ("Literacy" 341).

The Preston County women's schools had developed from one-room schools as late as the 1960s (Maddox and Maddox) to district elementary schools and then to consolidated high schools that drew from several elementary schools in their creeks and hollers. Schools were not bad, but they had little resources, little history, and an adult population with little formal education. Schools in town were generally considered better than those in the county, a division that continued until recently, since most professionals who settled in town had more education and income than did parents in the county.

In 1990, after these women had completed high school and enrolled in college, the Kentucky Education Resource Act was enacted to respond to the state's failing schools with a provision to equalize school systems, giving more funding to poorer districts than to school systems with a higher funding base. Even with reforms, the women worry that education for their children is not equal to other parts of the state, a concern supported by the fact that despite a large increase in adults who finished high school from 1970 to 1990, "Appalachia still lags [behind] the nation in educational attainment" (Isserman 4).

Many who do become college-educated leave the region because of lack of employment so that "domestic net out-migration of the college educated and workers in professional and scientific occupations depletes the state's human capital" and is a poor return on the investment the state has made in higher education (Price, Scobee, and Sawyer). In addition, the population of Preston County is declining, showing a 5 percent decrease in the last ten years (Kentucky Information Page).

Literacy rates relate to years of high school completed, and the Preston County women's age group—between the ages of twenty-five and forty-four—finished high school at the rate of 43 percent, compared to the men in their age group who graduated at 37 percent (Kentucky State Data Center). For many, then, achieving a high school diploma put them ahead of their class in more ways than one, and though women were encouraged to be literate, they had to be careful not to become too well educated, so many women chose not to attend college.

Choosing to attend college, then, was a big step for the Preston County women. While children in Baltimore and other urban areas who attend college generally have parents who are college-educated, these women grew up in homes where none of their parents had gone to college. In fact, six fathers of the eight women had not completed higher than an eighth-grade education because they had gone into the mines, whereas three of the eight mothers had completed high school. Among the eight Preston County women, Mary and Jean had dropped out—one in eighth grade, the other in tenth—because they got married and saw no further use for formal education. Sarah had good experiences in high school but postponed college until her son was in school; Lucy and Judith enrolled in college but dropped out after one semester; Faith enrolled and successfully completed an associate's degree and came to Preston College twenty years later; and Hope and Polly had neutral to negative experiences.

Once these women enrolled in college, some of them battled opposition: Lucy's illiterate husband would not allow schoolbooks in the house; Polly's relatives told her she should be at home taking care of the children; Hope's sisters-in-law gave her the silent treatment;

and Sarah's husband said that she needed to choose between the college and him. However, the women overcame these obstacles and joined a minority (5 percent) of women in their age group in the five-county region to finish a bachelor's degree (Kentucky State Data Center), an extraordinary feat.

In response to a question about women in education, Shannon, Jean's daughter, whom I interviewed to confirm Jean's influence on her life, observed:

> I think it's great that they're bringing more women into society now, and I think that women should be more independent. I think they should have the right, regardless of [whether] they work or not, to have the opportunity to go and reach a goal, reach for what they want. (April 15, 1999)

Naomi, Sarah's mother, suggested that every woman should have the chance for an education so that she doesn't have to depend on a man (April 30, 1999). Education provided these women with improved identity and bolstered their self-confidence.

Religion

Another difference we saw between Baltimore and eastern Kentucky was the prominence of religion. In Baltimore, we did not attend church because the ones in our neighborhood were large and cold. One of the first things we did when we moved to Preston was to attend St. Francis Catholic Church, since everyone attends church, and it was a good way to meet people. In addition to being part of a church, we found that every civic event, club meeting, and large gathering of people began proceedings with a call for prayer. The Southeast Bible College students read Bible stories weekly at the public schools until they were eventually challenged and removed. We heard "Christian" used to refer to attorneys, car dealers, and insurance salespersons. We learned that Christianity is central in the lives of Appalachian people and "[the people] are religious in the sense that most of [their] values and the meaning [they] find in life spring from the Bible. To understand mountaineers, one must understand [their] religion" (Jones, *Values* 39). But we also heard "Christian" being used as a social leveler; our children's babysitter's husband told us he was not a Christian and had been kicked out of a church because he drank beer occasionally. I soon learned about the distinctions that divide Old Regular, Freewill, and Primitive Baptists as well as the Church of Christ in its various tenets of faith, from one church believing, for example, that live music was the instrument of the devil to another that believed that organ and piano music was somehow permissible. I learned that some of these churches preached a pessimistic "social gospel [since] hard work did not always bring a sure reward" in this life, but the promise of "a sure reward in the hereafter" was more important (Dorgan 46).

The role of literacy in these churches appeared to be focused on women, because early in their history, some of the ministers, thinking seminary training unnecessary (all one needs is the call to preach from God), were untrained and nonliterates. The women in some of these churches could not preach, offer a blessing, wear makeup, cut their hair, or wear slacks, but they could write poetry and songs for the church, put songbooks together, or write obituaries for the annual church association in memory books (books listing tributes to church members who had died during the past year). Attending these churches, the women probably read the yearly church association minutes, information that included articles of faith, lists of member churches, meeting times, names of officers and visiting ministers, business meeting minutes, organization's history, and details of the election of elders ("St. Clair's").

Interviewing the women in this Preston County study, I found that the Bible was central to their early literacy whether they attended church or not, and they told stories of their grandmothers reading selections from the Bible to their husbands and family around the kitchen table, supporting Loyal Jones's observation that "ordinary people have dealt with the complexities of theology and use the Scriptures and lore from their culture to find meaning in life" (*Faith* 203).

Knowing how Christian the people of the region are, I was surprised when the Preston County women said that they had not attended church regularly since college. They found, as my friend

Candy did, that they would rather not attend church and have to face the dilemma of being challenged by family and church friends who believed in the literal interpretation of the Bible (Knudson). They may have also encountered churches that preached against education because it undermined and weakened the family, offering worldly "opportunities and enticements [which make people] more self-centered rather than family and church centered" (Jones, *Faith* 32–33).

As they became more educated, these mountain women began to question the fundamental religious beliefs they had grown up with. Mary, a study participant, spoke of how difficult it was for her to discuss what she was learning in classes with her mother and father, who were from "the old school and we were always taught things basically in black and white. I began to see more of the shaded areas and less of the black and white" from her freshman to her senior year in college (February 2, 1999). If these women went to church, they, like Jones's female Berea College students, tended "to join more liberal churches . . . as a means of dealing with changing ideas about gender roles" (Jones, *Faith* 205), though Sarah's mother, Naomi, pointed to the difficulty of finding a church that supports the independence of women. A woman who constantly read biblical commentaries, Naomi frequently argued with her minister, a person she described as nearly illiterate (April 30, 1999).

Having been raised Catholic in the South (and some mountaineers will insist that Catholics are not Christians), I found the gospel of the region's churches foreign—the Jesus I knew was full of love for sinners, and drinking did not qualify as a sin if it were done in moderation. So I was uncertain about the harsh message I heard, but I soon learned that thinking of God as loving is easy if a person's life is relatively free of stress and economic woes. Because they live a hard life, some mountain people see God in a more judgmental way. Sociologist Helen Lewis argues in an interview with Lori Briscoe and her colleagues that traits like "fatalism and passivity were not attributes of culture so much as defense mechanisms against exploitation and rapid social change" (164). I also began to realize that this worldview did not hold the region back, as some outsiders have claimed—there are too many factors causing poverty to blame it on one reason. Religion, then, like every other aspect of Appalachian life, replicated society at large in its class divisions, with working-class and lower-income people belonging to the more primitive churches and the middle and upper classes belonging to mainstream churches. Though organized religion may have lost some of its members, the women of this study had a new faith based on questioning their "old" religions, a faith that fit their belief in the power of women, a faith informed by reading and writing, a faith where everyone is responsible for exploring truth and can do that better if she is able to read and write (Bailey).

The Land

Religion's harsh message reflected the place, the land of the steep Appalachian mountains. Though people in general value the place in which they were born, many of us move away from that place (for me, Greensboro, North Carolina) and establish another set of neighbors and friends, some of whom become like family. Though we visit home when we can, the new town becomes our home. So when Mark and I moved to these mountains, we were unprepared for the attachment to place that we saw exhibited. The first question we were asked was, "Where are you from?" as local residents tried to discover our home place.

We learned that valuing place is "one of the unifying values of mountain people, and it makes it hard for us to leave the mountains" (Jones, *Values* 99). Jean, reflecting a consensus of the women participants, echoes Jones's sentiments: "It's hard to leave the area. It's like a security blanket, really. You know everybody and get along so well" (April 29, 1999). For Lucy, the comfort zone of the mountains contrasts with other places she has visited, and she dislikes "wide-open spaces." There are people who move away but who remain fiercely attached to the place where they grew up, traveling home regularly from places like Cincinnati, Detroit, and Akron for family events, holidays, and funerals. But though these women remained in the region, Sarah in her essay published in *Voices from the Hill* cautions me not to stereotype the area:

Many people feel close to their families but do move away for one reason or another. For example, I was brought up in a holler called Big Hackney's Creek. After I married Bill, we moved to Johns Creek to be near his job. Bill is a truck driver, and our living closer to his job makes it easier for him. We have made Johns Creek home for now. My Aunt Sheila grew up in the head of Grapevine. After her divorce, Sheila and her three kids moved to Florida, because she is an LPN and the wages are better there. She has made Florida home until something better comes her way. My friend Pamela was raised in a holler called Hen Roost. After she married her husband, Frank, she moved to West Germany. Frank is in the United States Air Force and is stationed there for three years. Germany will be Pamela's home until it is time to move again. (appendix F)

Being long-term residents of the region, we understand the attachment to the mountains, especially as the seasons change from barefaced winter trees outlining the hills to the white-blossomed service berry, dogwoods, and redbuds in the spring to lush summer foliage and flowers to the splendor of multicolored fall at eye level or above. On rainy and foggy days, smoky mists rest in mountain hollers. The sun does not come up until 10 A.M. in some places, and the sun may go down by 3 or 4, especially in the winter. Building is nearly impossible because the mountains are so steep, unlike the rolling Smokies and massive Rockies. A land of contrasts, the beauty of the mountains is scathed in spots by irresponsible mining and developers, and flooding may occur because of sediment in creek beds.

Steep mountains also mean slow driving with narrow or nonexistent road shoulders. For the first few years we were here, I feared driving the winding mountain roads, which doubled the time it took to go anywhere. After being able to travel the Baltimore beltway, I could not believe that traveling thirty miles might take up to an hour or longer if the traveler trailed a coal truck. To widen the roads and open the area up to commerce, millions of government and state dollars have been poured into the region because road contractors have had to literally move mountains to construct better roads. The Preston Cut-Through project took ten years and millions of dollars to cut through the mountain, re-route the river surrounding the town (thus preventing flooding in the town of Preston) and the train tracks running through the town, and expand the two-lane highway to four lanes. More recently at the Kentucky/Virginia state line, $44 million was spent to construct three miles of four-lane roads.

The steepness of the Appalachian Mountains has created a sense of physical isolation, though W. K. McNeil states that it is not any more isolated than other rural areas. Montgomery observes that isolation does not mean lack of culture or intelligence: "Far from being passive recipients of outside language and culture, mountain people have actively chosen and negotiated how much and what kind of interaction they want to have with the society at large" (12). The Preston County women are content to live in this region and remain close to their families, for they know, like Sarah, that "we've not had the drive-by shootings here at all. We are secluded from a lot of big-city violence" (May 5, 1999). While college education and upwardly mobility imply moving away from home to where graduate school and then employment opportunities are, the land has provided security and familiarity for the women so that they want to remain in its shelter. Perhaps they realize that

> local communities, regions, and histories are the places where we shape our individual lives . . . [and] it is at the local level where we are most able to act, and at the local level where we are most able to affect and improve community. (Brooke, *Rural* 4)

Mountain Values

The land has everything to do with the closeness of family in the region. When I asked the participants to define the area, they all concurred that close families was one of the positive stereotypes. Jean included her neighbors who lived in the same holler in her definition of family: "If they need something done, and you see them out working, and you know they haven't been feeling good, you'll go over and do it for them" (April 29, 1999). Living in the same holler where she grew up, Jean and her husband made a space for a trailer that belongs to her daughter, Shannon, and husband, Luther, behind their house. Lucy elaborated on the sense of security when she described how some families may live within five miles of one another:

> You've got brothers, sisters, mother, father, aunts, uncles, and grandparents living close to each other because when property was bought up, our ancestors bought it up in big lots. As the children left home, each child got a piece of that property, so they're all close to each other. (April 22, 1999)

The second question to strangers after "Where are you from?" is "Who are you related to?" During the first election after our arrival, we noticed that candidates listed their family lineage in newspaper ads. My neighbor and co-researcher, Connie, always signed her family name with her married name, not for any feminist purposes, as I had assumed, but because she wanted people to know her people. Mark and I learned quickly that family has a central place, and that was one of the main reasons that we were not invited to social events unless it was by other outsiders like those in our church. Mountain people are "more truly themselves when within the family circle" (Jones, *Values* 75), a place where they can present a "united front to the outside world" (Fiene 38). Relations who move away for jobs come home regularly, and at death they may be buried in the family plot located on the hills behind their homes.

That closeness is breaking down since people from the outside are moving into the area because of better roads and other opportunities. The holler that Lucy used to roam for hours with her brothers and sisters was at the time of the study too dangerous for her two children to explore since nonfamily neighbors had moved into the holler and were causing trouble with the law; "I stay right with them at all times" (April 22, 1999). Sarah also felt that the closeness of the area was changing. Formerly, she knew every neighbor in the holler where she grew up, but at the time of this study she knew just a handful. In the community she had moved to, all of the neighbors worked, so they did not have time for more than being courteous, and she was just as happy not to be close because she wanted her personal space (January 25, 1999).

Another value of the mountains that Mark and I have observed is modesty. Lucy earlier reflected that Appalachians are just like anyone else (April 22, 1999). She supports Jones's observation that "we mountaineers are levelers, and we believe we are as good as anybody else, but no better. We believe that we should not put on airs, not boast, nor try to get above our raising" (*Values* 90). One common phrase I heard from my students was "getting above your raisings," a phrase that generally refers to

> behavior that suggests a person is evaluating himself or herself as superior to family and close kin in the community. Speaking "proper," getting advanced education or exhibiting presumptive displays of wealth are some behaviors commonly associated with [the phrase]. (Puckett, *Seldom* 247)

This modesty precludes bragging about native talents or accomplishments. A form of this modesty occurs when people say yes to a request even if they never intend to grant it, just to avoid saying anything negative.

Being close to family and being modest can have detrimental effects on the women of the region if either keeps them from achieving their potential, insisting on their silence when they should be speaking. The Preston County women have apparently managed to defy cultural norms to finish college and use literacy to suit themselves and fit back into the fabric of their mountain lives.

Gender
After we moved here, I remember the shock of observing how stereotypically traditional married relationships were. I kept meeting strong women who bowed to their husband's directives on their activities. In my first job as Preston College continuing education

director, I had husbands call to make sure that their wives were attending the noncredit classes for which they had enrolled. When the first election came around, the Republican Party representative called and asked to speak to my husband, who was so registered, to determine how the household was voting, not even considering that I would vote differently. Having entered into marriage as an equal partner with my husband, I found this patriarchal model offensive and could not believe that women would accept a secondary role. When I scheduled an assertiveness training class the first year I lived in the region, I had only three people attend.

While this research certainly illustrated for me the power that threatened men can have in relationships with women, I have since learned that women who appear to be in traditional relationships often have more control than outward appearances would indicate. As mothers and caretakers, they figure centrally as the foundation of the Appalachian family, even when couples divorce. And though stereotypes of Appalachians have victimized men and women, there is a double bind for women, gender and class. When I asked these mountain women how they thought women from Appalachia were viewed, they mentioned the most common image of women barefoot and pregnant with a gun-toting husband sipping on a jug of moonshine, much like Ellie Mae in *The Beverly Hillbillies*, "voluptuous, vacuous, barefoot, and likely to be, if not already, pregnant. They tempt, confuse, and distract their menfolk, but they do not lead, instruct or direct the events that shape their lives" (Maggard 229). The Preston County women know the Appalachian arts of quilting, cooking, and poetry writing, and they also know how to maintain a garden and put food on their tables, but they resent the literature and media portrayal of mountain women as noble and long-suffering, "enigmatic but talented people who make beautiful quilts, spin wool into thread, weave it into coverlets, and play dulcimers in their spare time . . . quiet caretakers of an idealized mountain way of life" (229).

In fact, Appalachian women have other skills that make them strong, as illustrated by the persistent nurses at the local hospital who fought for ten years to get union rights (Maggard) and by the courageous women with whom Kathy Kahn, a community organization leader in the early 1970s, worked. Depicted in her book *Hillbilly Women* are women who have "blocked the giant bulldozers which still come to strip the land, destroy their mountains, and pollute their rivers. They have sheltered union organizers from company thugs. They have nursed starving children back to health" (xx).

In fact, women hold society together. They have been taught to bow to their husbands' wills, but many have learned to get their way by the back door. Their identity is tied to their central position as mothers, and they will fight with their husbands over their children, making a choice for the children in some cases. Mothers and daughters are particularly close. Though their rhetoric was feminist in many cases, the Preston County women themselves resist the feminist label because they believe that they can confront those with whom they disagree in a more agreeable and subtle way. Hepzibah Roskelly, acknowledging her "redneck" heritage, admits that "rural southerners know when to get angry and when not to show it. . . . It's a flaw to 'show yourself,' the redneck term for thinking so highly of yourself that you might cause others inconvenience" (304). Mountaineers frequently use humor, which "allows [them] to resist what they do not agree with, avoid direct conflict, keep their dignity and self-respect, and have a little fun, too" (Jones, *Values* 6). Mary Anglin in her anthropological research talks about how "backtalking" operates for Appalachian laborers resisting poor working conditions: they hold worship services next to mines or confront supervisors in congenial terms. When people here feel insulted, they won't necessarily disagree openly, but their response will "devil" their opponents if they are really listening.

Academic literacy enabled these women to get the job training or skills improvement that they needed in order to make a living wage for their families, like the women in Virginia Seitz's community study. Cultural and family role expectations of "mother-protector" and caretaker in male-dominated families persisted while they were in college, but they, like the women in Marcia Egan's research, demonstrated choice, control, and perseverance to choose school over family. After graduation, they felt a sense of confidence, influenced directly by their teachers. Education continues to be a concern for the region, but these women have taken matters into their own hands and made better lives for themselves and their families.

Summary

When I look back on all that I have learned from the first day we drove into town in our trusty Dodge Charger some thirty years ago, I am thankful. Much has changed in the region since my impression of Preston as a dark coal town at the end of civilization's road. More aware now of how the region has been victimized, I resist the urban orientation of the media that depicts as ignorant anyone who chooses to live beyond the city limits. I especially resist those who set the standard against which the rest of the nation is defined, promoting the belief that nonstandard speakers lack intelligence. I believe with Garret Keizer that "without the manure pile there can be no universities, no cathedrals, no theaters, no museums, no shopping malls" (23) and that rural areas nourish humanity and provide diversity, contributing to a "pluralist and regional rather than nationalist" orientation (Shapiro xix). Appalachia contributes to the diversity of our nation with its differences and similarities to other groups. Ultimately, living in the region has taught me about the dignity of work and the value of the people who stay because of their attachment to the land, their churches, and their families and communities.

When I look back on the time my family has lived here and the blessing of the people who have embraced us and enriched our lives, I am grateful, but most especially for the gift the eight women from Preston County gave me of their time and trust. Though place-bound, their stories represent the stories of women in all regions of the country who have to battle adversity to go to college. In the chapters that follow, Lucy, Jean, and Sarah expand this Appalachian story as they demonstrate "the rhetoric of life beyond the classroom": the interaction between reading, writing, and self (McAndrew).

3 / The Literacy Practices of Lucy
Reading Her World

Graduating from Preston College in 1996 with a degree in art, Lucy represented the average academic student among the three case studies. So that she could take care of her two children—Bud, a second grader at the time of this study, and Sally, her two-and-a-half-year-old daughter born with cystic fibrosis—she was not employed outside the home. I almost did not get the chance to interview Lucy because she missed two appointments; later I ran into her at the grocery store. Immediately apologetic, Lucy said she had missed our latest meeting because she had driven her mother to a central Kentucky medical appointment, but she would be happy to meet with me the following week. Although each case study interview was unique, Lucy's story awakened me to the multiple effects of literacy, the importance of expressivist writing for nontraditional students, and the redefinition of what literacy means beyond college. As I have done in each of the case studies that follow, I developed Lucy's extended narrative by combining her interview statements. I will interrupt that narrative between sections to comment on her story.

> I am Lucy. I am an open book, the person in the doctor's office who will tell you her life story and carry on a conversation. They tell you about their family, their dogs or cats, and everything else. If this book is made into a TV movie, I want Michelle Pfeiffer to play my part, though I am a large woman, dark-headed and wearing black-rimmed glasses. You will generally always see a smile on my face.

My dad's family was one of the founding families of Preston County in 1850, and we were successful recently getting the new public golf course named after the patriarch of that family, William. My mother, child of a German mother and Cherokee father and raised on a North Carolina reservation, taught me crafts and sewing, skills I use now to make my own and my children's clothes. I never got to know her parents because we weren't that close, and they lived so far away.

Like other eastern Kentucky families, my dad's grandparents bought up land in one holler, so I grew up surrounded by them and their children, my aunts and uncles. That closeness is changing now, and I am much more careful since my aunt moved away and sold her house to strangers who just recently were raided by the police for drugs. I will not let my children roam the hills as I once did.

The story of my family reads like a novel. We grew up poor, though I never felt that way. My dad finished high school. My grandfather worked for the gas company, a good job in those days. Dad attended vocational school and worked as a mine electrician and then as a salesman, delivery man, and an all-around fix-it guy. My mother finished eighth grade and while I was growing up held restaurant jobs, did housecleaning, and worked as an aide in the Office of Economic Opportunity program. Our family was large, and we did not have much. If we wanted to use the phone, we went to my grandfather's house, though most of Preston County did not have phone service until the early

'70s. If we wanted to watch TV, we had to rig up a metal antenna at the top of the mountain behind our house to get three stations.

As the middle of seven children (the good one, the neglected one), I remember almost idyllic times with my siblings, leaving after breakfast, running up and down the creek, helping in the garden, making stone soup from rocks in the creek bed, and not returning home until supper time. We had no running water and no electricity, so we had to burn coal and carry our water. We eventually had electricity, but we never did have running water unless, as we joked, we ran up the hill and back down to get it.

Pre-college Literacy

Lucy elaborated on her models of literacy during her childhood and in the years before she attended college.

I grew up seeing my parents read *Reader's Digest,* the weekly (now triweekly) newspaper, and the Bible. Mother read books and detective magazines and wrote poems and songs. She took us to church in the same holler where we lived and where she taught Sunday school regularly; reading the Bible figured centrally in our family life.

Attending public school was not a positive experience for me. Our teachers were from "generational" families, ones whose mothers and aunts and uncles were teachers as well. They had to teach me, and that's basically the only relationship I had with them. Every day in sixth grade, I remember my teacher would have something to say about my clothing: "Well, it looks like Lucy left her skirt at home and wore her shirt," and other such comments. It was like that all the way through school. When I transferred briefly to the town school, the teachers and students treated me worse, so I got into fights. I have always been large, and our family with seven kids has always been poor, and the teachers had no use for me or my family. Though they never discouraged me, they had their little special kids to pay attention to.

During my high school years, I wrote poetry and short stories at home, but I do not remember ever writing an essay in school. In elementary school, I went to the school library once a week and wrote book reports. I did well in mathematics, but I always had a reading problem. Still, I made C grades and graduated from high school, which none of my other siblings had done. To help out with family expenses, I worked full-time from the age of sixteen in a major retail chain, advancing from department to department and ending up as head cashier.

Though I did average work in high school, the Preston College Upward Bound and Talent Search came to our high school and asked my brother Marty and me to be part of their summer program. I attended college immediately after high school, but I dropped out the second semester of my freshman year. My grandfather was ill, and I loved taking care of him. I was still working, but to tell you the truth, I was flunking several subjects, and I quit before they asked me to leave. I met my husband, Matt, and we decided to get married, followed soon afterwards by the arrival of our son, Bud. My pay was still minimum wage and barely

enough to support us since my husband did not work, so
I knew I would have to return to college to get a better job.
Ten years after my first try at Preston College, I returned.

Listening to Lucy's narrative, I was curious about the education of her parents, as well as the parents of the other Preston County women, since a college education is usually modeled by at least one parent. None of the parents of the Preston County women completed college. The fact that Lucy's father completed high school was rare because men frequently had to drop out to go into the mines to support their families. His enrollment in vocational school was also important. That her mother finished eighth grade fits with the regional data, which show that 51–80 percent of the participants' parents' generation (between the ages of fifty-five and seventy-five) rarely finished ninth grade, whereas the women's generation improved to better percentages (Kentucky State Data Center).

Her description of indifferent to hostile teachers during her public school years made me more aware of how working-class students experience education. As the parent of two children who went through the Preston city school, I know how public schools channel college-bound students with advanced placement courses and the like, so that most average to poor students like Lucy see college beyond their reach, which reinforces class differences even further. Despite her "generational" teachers who discriminated against her because of her class, Lucy did not fail any subjects and averaged C grades, doing well in mathematics. Her elementary school literacy focused on book reports she wrote, but she disliked reading. If she were in school currently, she might be diagnosed with a special learning problem and be given more help with her reading in elementary and secondary school. If reading created problems for her, teachers may have shunted her aside to deal with the better students. The Preston College federally funded Upward Bound program, with goals to encourage students to be the first in their families to attend college, must have seen her potential and invited her to join the program.

Lucy's public school experience resonates with other literacy studies examining working-class students in public schools. One of Virginia Seitz's informants in her study of Appalachian community organizations states, "I didn't know I was poor white trash until I went to school and somebody told me. If I had never gone to school, I never would have known I was poor!" (120). In *Coal Miners' Wives: Portraits of Endurance,* one of Carol Giesen's participants speaks in a similar vein: "I couldn't buy books, and I was ashamed because I didn't have clothes like the other children had" (25). Experiences like Lucy's "sever . . . society and slice . . . opportunities and rights of its poorest people" by reinforcing class divisions and excluding working-class people from the process (Stuckey 118). In fact, Seitz's respondents felt that the school system perpetuated the stereotypes of working-class students by ignoring them and tracking them "from the academic and social environment of the schools into low-wage service jobs" (119). The effect on women like Lucy was that it made them "doubt their own value, voice, and abilities" (Luttrell 113–14). The promises of schooling to improve lives did not generally impress these women, since "without major changes on a national level . . . they [working-class people] would most likely simply move from one sector of working poor to another" (Merrifield et al. 98). Lucy and women like her managed to overcome public school experiences as they enrolled in college.

College Literacy

However, for women in other literacy studies of adult education and college women (Bingman; Luttrell; Horsman; Merrifield et al.; Pascall and Cox; Lunneborg), education outside the public school setting offered new opportunities and a glimmer of hope, allowing them "a new sense of themselves and what they might be able to do with their lives" (Bingman 217). With the encouragement of her parents, who were literate models for her, though they did not attend college, and with the determination that characterizes the women in these literacy narratives, Lucy enrolled at Preston College.

Because I like working with people, I thought when I enrolled in Preston College for the second time that I wanted to prepare for a career in social services. But I took my first college art class and exclaimed to myself, "This is what I am here for!" I loved working with my hands to draw, paint, and sculpt. The reason art was so appealing is that I'm better at doing something with my hands, though listening helps in class lectures. I am not a big reader, so I get more out of something by having someone tell me what it says rather than me actually reading it.

Writing for school was new to me, so I struggled with getting the right format and using the right verbs and spelling. I used spell-check when I was at the college, and I still couldn't get it right. The word was so badly misspelled. I thought that I must be dyslexic or something because I even read words wrong. English was hard, but my English background is not so good anyway. I passed the writing proficiency exam the first time I took it and earned a C for the class. However, English 112 was a different story. I'd never done a research paper before college, I had a hard time finding a topic, and I am lazy. If you do research papers, you have to read, which I hate, so I received a D.

Finding something to write about in English 111 was no problem for me with all the adventures of my large family. I enjoy telling a story and found writing stories a good outlet for me. Besides English class, I wrote a research paper on an artist for art history and essay exams in other subjects.

Lucy's discovery of art as a way to express her creativity connected well with what I found out later permeated her post-college literacy in the display of her paintings in her trailer. In addition, she designed and sewed clothing for herself and her family. As she says, majoring in art allowed her "to draw, paint, and sculpt," to realize her natural talent, creativity she may have inherited from her mother. Like the other women's choice of majors, Lucy reflected the need for education to be immediately concrete and "hands-on." Unlike the other participants, Lucy chose a way to express herself unbounded by words and reminds us that too much emphasis on spoken and written language "fails to consider the full range of experience" conveyed in the "musical, mathematical, or visual nature" of communication (Boone and Mignolo 7).

The same creativity expressed itself in her essays in composition class. Personal writing was a natural vehicle for Lucy in spite of her spelling problems; it allowed her to be "the open book" to which she refers in the beginning of this chapter. Her process essay, "Marty and Me," was nominated and accepted by the editor of the 1992–93 edition of *Voices from the Hill* (see appendix D). A required text for the composition sequence, the paperbound booklet published by the English department was based on the concept that students learn more from each other's essays than from published authors' works in most composition readers. Below is an excerpt from Lucy's paper in which she and brother Marty prepared to clean the bees out of a neighbor's corncrib:

> The bees were everywhere, filling the sky like a dark cloud.
> "OH, MY GOD!" Marty yelled as he grabbed the smoke gun and began puffing out the smoke towards the angry bumblebees, but there was no effect. . . . Soon all the bees were out of the corncrib and ready for war.
> Then I felt the sharp, warm sting of a bee to my ear and to the back of my neck. I suddenly realized with horror that the bumblebees had gotten under my net. I began to scream in pain, "Help me, Marty! Help me! They're in my hat." "Hold still!" he yelled as he grabbed a horseweed out of the ground. . . . By the time he got to me, I was halfway down the hill, and all my gear was lying on the hill behind me.

She finishes the story by saying that the cost of ointments and bandages for bee stings were not worth the $15 the neighbor paid them and that he would have to do his own work the next time. Her use of quotations and building up of suspense with good detail in this essay conveys her talent as a natural storyteller. She passed the proficiency exam given at the end of English 111 and earned a C for the class.

As she reports above, she didn't do as well in English 112, the research class, which she attributed to her poor reading skills, a carryover from high school. Her analysis of her reading interested me: she did well with short, magazine-length articles, but books intimidated her, and she preferred to watch movies based on books, another use of literacy. One of the appeals of majoring in art and using her hands was the de-emphasis on reading. She liked lecture classes because she could listen and take notes, but she disliked classes that required more reading.

More remarkable than any of Lucy's past literacy experiences was what she had to confront daily when she left the college classroom.

> One of the reasons I liked working with my hands in art was that it kept my mind off the abusive situation at home. In fact, college was my getaway place, and I hated to leave at the end of the day because I had to face my husband, Matt. Well, I guess you could say that he was the model for the stereotype many outsiders have of the region. He was born in a nearby county where men control everything women do. They want to make sure that the women do not do anything unless they say so. But they don't want to work. It tickles the man to death if the wife has a job and supports him. They call him and men like him "go-getters." He drops his wife off at work in the morning and "goes to get her" when she finishes work.

He "allowed" me to go to college but only if he drove me there and back and if I kept my schoolbooks in the car. I would usually lie to him and tell him I had to be there an hour or two earlier, so I'd have time to go to a quiet place and study and do what I had to do. Then he would pick me up. If my class work didn't get done, then I couldn't do it at home. If I had to study for a test, I could not stay up all night like other students. While I was at school, Matt traded knives, toys, jewelry, and furniture. He couldn't read and write, and he could barely write his name. I don't know if he thought I was going to outgrow him or what, but he just didn't see the need of education. He didn't want any reading and writing material in the house, no magazines, and certainly none of my schoolbooks. I had to do house-cleaning or take care of our son, Bud, who was not in school at that time. Matt even objected to my parents' caring for Bud while I was in class but made no effort himself to care for the child. In fact, he wouldn't even stay in the same room when the child ate.

During my college years, there was one particularly abusive weekend after I had found out that he had been cheating on me, and I confronted him. And I went through thirty hours of abuse—yelling, screaming, and hitting. He even used a knife. That Monday, I dropped by to see my adviser, Elena, who noticed how upset I was. She contacted the campus minister who helped me get a restraining order, because during this time and later there were incidents. They also contacted a pro bono lawyer who helped me get a divorce. Two years later, Matt died of cirrhosis of the liver.

Looking back, I believe that his alcohol abuse, illness, and ignorance compounded to make life difficult for him and, as a result, for me and Bud.

Trouble seems to follow me. In my senior year, I fell in love with a man and became pregnant with Sally, my youngest. He and I were carriers for cystic fibrosis, so she was born with the disease. We decided it was not a good idea to get married, so I am raising my Bud and Sally by myself.

Laughing when she told me about Matt modeling the stereotype outsiders have of mountain men, Lucy's life with Matt was no laughing matter. In fact, she cried openly when she related the scenario in her adviser's office. Lucy's story woke me up to the possible destructive nature of literacy, challenging me as a teacher. Though she had told me when she was in my class that her husband did not support her being in school and I had offered her the opportunity of extended deadlines for assignments if she needed it, I had not gone any further with my questions, with help. Though I have been aware—usually from their journal entries—that some of my female students were being abused and have referred them to shelters, Lucy's cheerful manner had led me to believe that the objections Matt raised were only superficial. I certainly never could have imagined that his nonsupport extended so radically to the point of not allowing her to bring schoolbooks into the house and physically abusing her. Where were my listening ear and powers of observations? In spite of its promises that I had bought into, literacy can be a two-edged sword that "generates increasing tension between husband and wife, within families, and between friends, as gender roles are unmasked in their grimness, and as alternatives are highlighted in literature and theory" (Lauer xii). The incident reported in her art adviser's office the year after she took my class showed me the importance of small college faculty; students feel free to come for help. If faculty cannot help, they can make referrals.

Though no one else among the participants reported physical abuse, others experienced negative reactions from their families.

Sarah reported that her husband thought "he was the man and he was the care provider, he should take care of everything. . . . So when I started college, it was [as if] he felt that it was a threat to him and his manhood in providing for his family" (January 25, 1999). Polly's family and Jean's mother and father-in-law thought these women could not possibly go to college and do justice to raising children at home. Hope's sisters-in-law gave her the silent treatment. Women are not supposed to whistle or crow; those who objected were threatened by these women's growth and change.

Their stories reminded me of a similar case study of community college student Marnie, who overcame drug and spouse abuse to attend college. Though Matt, Lucy's husband, was not destructive of her books, Marnie's nonsupportive husband "would rip up my books, put them in the toilet, keep me up all night fighting so I would be too tired to concentrate in class the next day" (qtd. in S. Rodriguez 5). Still, college offered Marnie a chance to move from low self-esteem to self-confidence and graduation.

While abuse is not acceptable in any sense, I cannot create false dichotomies by making Lucy's or Marnie's husband the "bad guys." Though his actions hurt Lucy, Matt was probably a victim himself of poverty and the school system geared to average or above-average middle- or upper-class students. Although literacy professionals know that many people of limited literacy do not necessarily lead "impoverished lives" and are frequently more competent and functional than one might expect (Merrifield et al. 3), as a researcher I do not know enough about her husband's personal literacy and strategies for learning and surviving. If he grew up in poverty, he may have been alienated from the education system and was not encouraged to finish school. He probably knew how little education and its benefits affected people like him. What can literacy professionals do to overcome this feeling of shame, "the trappings of backwardness," which lack of education instills (Villanueva, personal communication)? Is Lucy's husband one of the many in the academic classroom whose isolation led to his lack of cultural knowledge and who was blamed for his personal deficiency and put out to pasture (Geissenger et al.)? Other men in the region did not finish high school because they saw no reason for it and needed to earn money for their families. Men may be trapped in a life that is not always of their choice, especially if they are the primary breadwinners, and like the miners in Giesen's work, "It was school or food on the table, and what choice was there?" (26).

Matt's response and the negative responses of the families of the Preston County women may also have occurred because of a strong religious upbringing, which sees women's place in the home and that more and better education is divisive of the family and hence evil. It is connected to the fear I spoke of earlier of becoming educated and being severed from their families. Since most of the eight women reported that education helped them see the gray areas of issues that used to be black and white and since many no longer attended the church they grew up in, a natural part of faith and educational development, their parents' fears may have had some basis, though not to the extent they had imagined.

Finally, I cannot know what harbored the fear that made Matt order Lucy to keep her books in the car and not allow printed material in the house, drink so excessively, and abuse her. Though I do not condone his making Lucy suffer, to dismiss him as the enemy is shortsighted.

Women like Lucy blunt the edges of the literacy sword by taking charge of their lives and acquiring skills that enable them to stand on their own. College transformed Lucy's life and made her aware of other vistas. Her resiliency reminded me of several transformation stories, notably Sharon Jean Hamilton's; she described herself as a disobedient, uneducable, and socially maladjusted person until adopted by her stepmother who exposed her to literacy, which equipped her with "knowledge and confidence to decide how I would live my life as the kind of person I wanted to be" (xiv). Marnie, referred to above, overcame her own drug abuse and divorced her abusive and nonsupportive husband to graduate from college. In fact, it is possible that women can use traumatic relationships like Lucy's with fathers or husbands to "spark and strengthen [their] determination to get a college degree and professional status" (Hammons-Bryner 14). For the African American women in

S. Hammons-Bryner's study, "education [was] the main avenue for escaping dependence on men, a situation that they viewed as unpleasant and undesirable" (14). Like Lucy, the women who experience the two-edged nature of literacy generally end up divorcing their husbands and moving away from the abusive situation, strengthened with the skills and self-confidence they have gained from college.

Post-college Literacy

Since the focus of my research was literacy practices since college, I asked all the participants about how they were using literacy in the home and workplace. Since Lucy did not work outside the home, I did my observation in her home, which is located in a holler on the right fork of Bullpen Creek on a narrow, windy mountain road whose mouth (the beginning of the holler; the end of the holler is the "head") is about a mile off the four-lane state road. Her trailer sat between her mom and dad's trailer and another trailer they keep as a guest house for any family member who needs it. Hers has brand-new tan siding, which she got after extensive water damage was done to the trailer. Toys and animals surrounded her home. From this observation and our follow-up interview, Lucy shared these thoughts about her use of literacy.

Literacy for Disease Management

I graduated in May 1996 and in August gave birth to Sally, who was born with the serious genetic disease cystic fibrosis, something which has dramatically changed my life. The first two years of her life I spent traveling to the University Hospital (about three hours from Preston) where I found a pediatric pulmonologist who knows about current treatments. My parents kept Bud during this time. In addition to nine hospital visits for stays of two or more weeks at a time during that year, I learned to provide respiratory treatments for Sally five times a day. I worry about Sally's future since the average age for children with this disease to survive is 30.1 years. Since her care is too complicated for anyone else to do, I choose not to work outside the home, even if I were physically able to do so.

Once I became pregnant, I spent hours learning about the disease. Before Sally was born, I called the Cystic Fibrosis Foundation, who sent me stacks of information on CF, including a monthly newsletter which I still receive. So I did a lot of reading. Now I have the large notebook which the pulmonologist gave me, full of information on the disease and its treatment. In the book are words and pictures showing how to perform the process of tapping [percussion] on the lungs of a CF patient and all the breathing treatments which have to be done four to six times a day. In addition to cystic fibrosis, Sally also has epileptic seizures, so she needs as many as twenty-nine different kinds of pills.

When Sally was first born, I kept a journal of when she ate and what she ate because when she eats, she has to take medication to digest the food since her digestive system doesn't work properly either. The doctor helps me manage the disease and warns me of the complications once Sally goes to school, where she will be exposed to more germs and diseases. I will not let him give Sally experimental drugs for a cure until they are proven safe, since I would rather lose Sally through the disease's natural process than to have her die from an experimental drug.

Knowing the frustrations of raising a CF child, I tried

to organize a support group for parents of children with cystic fibrosis by finding out their names and calling them, but no one was interested. No one wants to get together. I've tried. I even talked to the health department about starting a support group. I don't know why, either, since it's not contagious or anything. The other CF parents just don't want to talk about it.

Lucy's use of literacy to manage her child's disease is exemplary of her natural curiosity and her concern for her daughter. Even before Sally was born, Lucy wanted to read as much as possible to prepare herself, though she had earlier stated how much she hated reading. Once again this confounds the narrow definition of good reading, often given by academics as reading good literature. By her own admission, reading is a problem, though she states that she spends most of the day reading something. Keeping a journal also helped her with disease management, which became routine after awhile. She was concerned about the effect of Sally's illness on her son, who also lost his dad during that time, especially because Sally's first year of life was filled with emergency visits to the university hospital, three hours away. Her parents kept Bud during that time to relieve her concern. Self-preservation entered into her reaction to the doctor's proposal of experimental drugs; recipients of supplementary payments like Lucy are often guinea pigs for experiments. More impressive to me was her initiative to gather CF parents together to form a support group. The lack of response from other parents could have reflected a general difficulty at that time in organizing other support groups in the region because of the sense of independence and individualism that characterizes some Appalachians who consider the family their support group. Not content to give up, however, she recently wrote a letter to the editor after her child had to suffer the ignorance of classmates about her disease (see appendix G) and had a recent newspaper article written about her efforts to organize a walkathon for cystic fibrosis.

Personal Literacy

As far as reading goes, I am one of those kinds of people that try to look for the movie that goes with the book, though I am a sucker for sobby stories like those in *Reader's Digest*. I am not a real good reader. I never did like to read because my mind wanders. I start reading, and I just wander off and lose the page. I think, "Well, how would I have written this?" I'm real critical when I'm reading. When I read things, I try to go to the key point. I don't want the build-up, the introduction. I don't read books because I don't get anything out of them. I miss what the author's doing, trying to figure out what I would do. So I just don't try. Stories like a recent story in the newspaper about a thirteen-year-old victim of cancer who had written a book about his ordeal touch me. I read as little as possible, mainly magazines, newspapers, the Bible, the newsletter about CF progress, and instructions on medication or how to do other things.

I read recipes since I love to cook, especially for my friends. Since I love soap operas, I subscribe to and read *Soap Opera Digest*. I also read *Reader's Digest* to which my parents in the trailer next door subscribe and the *Appalachian News Express,* the local triweekly paper.

In addition to my reading and writing, I express myself in art, using paint and clay. I have several oil paintings from college on the walls of my trailer: an oil painting entitled *Broken Promises* features a cloth in a jar with masks around, one broken apart. Another watercolor depicts a little boy with a big fishing hat, and another painting on the living room wall is a still life of a child's clothes and shoes. I also have a beautiful sculpted pink and beige clay angel, which I always packed with Sally's belongings on our many hospital trips the first year of her life. I prefer free-handed sculpture, but with my arthritis, those projects take longer than they used to. Bud's drawings and schoolwork sit next to my work.

Observing Lucy's literacy artifacts in her home, I learned about the complexities of literacy. Knowing the primacy of the Bible in her own literacy education, I was not surprised to see three different Bibles in the house, including a new one that she told me her son had won at an Easter egg hunt at his school held by the Christian Appalachian Project. The bookshelf located in Bud's room housed most of her books and materials with the exception of her journals, sketchbooks, and papers, which she was storing elsewhere until the trailer renovation was complete. The contents revealed literacy events in Lucy's life and illustrated the literal and figurative vertical accumulation of literacy over the years (Brandt, "Accumulating"). Left over from her college days were texts that she reported she consulted occasionally and two copies of the Preston College English handbook. A coffee table book, *Mountain Worlds,* the gift of one of her sisters so Lucy could paint a picture for her from it, sat next to those books.

There were children's books, crossword puzzle books, a home remedy book, and blank college notebooks that her son and daughter scribbled in. Knowing about her self-described trouble with spelling, I grinned at the book *Gateway to Spelling,* recognizing her attempt to overcome her spelling problem. In addition to high school and college yearbooks, the shelves contained videos (*Charlotte's Web* and other action-type movies) and computer games next to books that, Lucy reported, the school gave the children at different times during the school year.

Observing her literacy, I was amazed that she described herself as a nonreader when she was an avid reader of materials for her daughter's illness, the local newspaper, and the popular press. When

I asked her how she defined a literate person, she focused on the reasons people become educated, but her other responses conveyed to me a sense of inferiority when it came to reading, though in every way I would define Lucy as literate.

Literacy for Household Maintenance and Communication

I pay bills on the first of the month at my kitchen table before the social security check comes out on the third of the month. I keep my receipts in a box at the top of Sally's dresser along with prescription receipts. I regularly jot down events on a calendar like doctor's appointments and birthdays, and I keep a journal of special events that happen to me and my children, like reflecting on my son, Bud, being away at camp for the first time. Like my mother, I love to write poetry and short stories and had a poem published in a vanity press which wanted $99 for a copy of the book which contained the poem. Needless to say, I do not own a copy of that book. The local newspaper has also published some of my poems. I regularly write letters to Sally's half-sister in California but communicate by phone with my sisters who live in other parts of the state.

I get fired up easily about issues and have written many letters to the editor of our local paper to vent my feelings. One issue which upset me was deadbeat dads, particularly my sister's ex-husband who was refusing to support their child. He was married to somebody else at the same time, so he had to go for blood tests, and he refused. So they had a trial, and the jury said that it was his daughter, and he would have to pay. So he paid $50 a month, and he was nine years behind. The situation made me so angry that I fired off a letter to the paper. I am one of those people that if something inspires me, at THAT moment, I'll get real heated and I'll write something, and then I'll calm down about it afterwards. Then I will send it later if I think it will help.

Lucy's use of literacy permeated her life, most notably in her journal. Her short observations about her son being away point to her conflict in seeing him independent and missing him (see figure 2). In addition, I see more and more of her letters to the editor of the local newspaper, which I had not noticed before this study. Though they are not part of the original research, I include two of these letters as artifacts in appendix G. At the time of this writing, she had been elected to the Site Based Council of her son and daughter's school, and so one letter refuted the community's negative response to the condition of the school, and the other challenged middle-income parents who drive their children to school and back traffic up on the highway instead of using the school bus. Though there are no misspellings, probably because the editor has cleared those up, Lucy composes the letters well, using humor, sarcasm, and examples to illustrate her points.

Lucy's home literacy reminded me of Shirley B. Heath's Roadville residents (who have Appalachian roots) whose typical uses of writing were to remember items and events, to keep account of finances, and to interact with others through cards, letters, and e-mails (*Ways* 218). Her participants in Roadville actively wrote letters and sent cards, but Heath makes no mention of letters to the editor, which I feel lies within another genre. David Barton and Mary Hamilton's informants used letters to effect social change, and though she is only one person, Lucy was setting out to effect some kind of change in these letters.

Reading the System: Family

When my daughter was diagnosed with cystic fibrosis, I knew that medical bills would be high, and I did not have health insurance. Yet I was able to secure complete medical

JUNE 14, 1999
Bud left for camp today, his first time away. I think maybe he might not stay the whole week. Sally misses him already. Another day of potty training going well.

JUNE 15, 1999
Called Bill—he said Bud got to camp ok. I have to admit I miss Bud too and I'm a little worried. Sally's first day of potty training—no accidents.

JUNE 16, 1999
Cleaned Buds room—took all day. Sally helped—she misses Bud a lot. Took Sally to play with Brian; they fought the whole time.

JUNE 17, 1999
Same old Same old.

JUNE 18, 1999
Called Kathy about making Nadia's shower cake. They decided on a double heart (make note—need to practice).

JUNE 19, 1999
Bud came home from camp. He had a great time so much so he wants to go back. I missed him more than he missed me. He was invited back for the 5-10 July. He is already packing to go back. I'm glad he had a good time but he could of missed me a little more. Sally was glad to see her brother but as I write he is tormenting her. Oh to the wonderful sounds of screaming children!

JUNE 20, 1999
Took the kids out to eat after church. potty train has been a success. Now I need to order her a trophy. I promised.

Fig. 2. Lucy's journal entries, June 1999

coverage for her hospitalization. In addition, I have health problems, so I had to fight to get social security benefits. The fight is not easy. The government fixes the laws so that you've got to pay someone to go to bat for you. I think it's because lawmakers are lawyers. It's big business because 80 percent of everyone who applies to social security automatically gets turned down, meaning that they must hire an attorney to get the judgment reversed. To recover my benefits, I hired an attorney known for working with social security claims. For him, I filled out the necessary forms, went to doctors recommended by the Social Security Administration to determine my eligibility, and attended a hearing where the judge asked me about my health and physical limits. After that, my attorney brought in some medical terms, and that was it. He did not do a whole lot of work but charged me $4,000. After the attorney's fee, I received $12,000, which I used to make needed repairs on the house and purchase a new car so that I did not have to depend on others for transportation.

I receive a social security and Medicaid check for Sally's cystic fibrosis and a disabled social security and Medicaid check for her hospital expenses. Any other costs are also covered by supplemental payments. Because I also have medical problems, I draw a check, as does my son, Bud. During college, I got AFDC [Aid to Families with Dependent Children], which was $197 a month, and that's all I got since after the divorce, my ex-husband was not paying child support.

Another program sponsored by the local mental health agency which I learned about was a program which provided playground equipment if a doctor certified need for a child. I was able to get a brand new swing set and other toys for my children. Since I can't afford it on my own, this benefit enabled me to afford useful play toys. These same folks helped me with medical equipment and transportation as well.

Reading the System: Community

Since I do not work outside the home, I use my time helping others. My minister's wife has been depressed lately, and I thought that doing art projects might help her, so I started reading about art therapy programs. I am teaching craft classes at our church for the women. I sew costumes and my own clothes since I am such a large person. One dress I made recently had 100 sequins hand-sewn on the front. I usually take a pattern and adjust it to my frame. I also mend and sew new clothes for my children, relatives, and friends. I bake cakes for friends and family. For my friends at the Mine Health and Safety Administration, I recently designed and painted symbols on their hard hats.

Recently, I helped a close friend of the family in her twenties who had lost her trailer in a fire. I called the Hope Center, which provides food and clothing, and they said all they needed was a copy of the fire department report. I called Wal-Mart, and they said all she needed to do was to come to the store and fill out a request. I put together fruit baskets, decorate cakes, sing in the choir, and assist at funerals and weddings.

Reading the System: Lucy's Children's School

Having battled "generational" teachers as a student, I know

how to work through the system so that Bud doesn't have to suffer the same. I spend time with Bud's teachers and get upset when teachers are unfair. One of his teachers was trying to make the children sell Avon products for her, so I called the county school board to report her since I thought it was unfair, especially for parents who don't have the money. They need a better class of teachers because in my son's school, there are still the generation teachers all over again. My children are not getting the quality that places away from here get. The teachers they have are over-worked because they have large classrooms of children. Besides all of that, the principal at our school defends his teachers before he believes what parents had to say.

A creative person, Lucy reads the system primarily to help her family, then to help others in the community, and finally to challenge the school system so that her son does not have to experience what she did. Her generosity is impressive considering that she lives on a fixed income and confounds a class perception of government-subsidized recipients as passive and selfish. When I asked her if she charged for any of her work, she said she would never consider it; these were friends and relatives. Most important, Lucy's knowledge of the system and her literacy enabled her to get help for her young friend as she acted in the role of what Barton and Hamilton call "local expertise," a term used to describe "people who become experts through their sense making activities . . . to have their specialised area of knowledge" (243). This literacy event, securing help for neighbors, "calls for appropriate knowledge of forms [like the fire department report] and uses of speech events" and shows how spoken and written language are "integral to the nature of participants' interaction and interpretive process" (Heath, "Protean" 350). Since she herself has to fight for benefits, Lucy knows the ways of finding help for others. I believe that Lucy's college education gave her the confidence to see herself as more capable so that she could challenge the authorities (her son's school, the board of education, social security) and become "a critical user of literacy, to us[e] literacy in an empowering way" (Barton and Hamilton 245). Literacy enhanced her natural sense of justice for herself and others and reminded me of Ellen Cushman's informants who used their communicative skills to work with gatekeepers to show how "power emerges in everyday interactions" (xii).

Another system that Lucy reads is the school her son (and now daughter) attends. What most impressed me was her aggressive involvement in the school when her own public school experience was so bad; most parents with poor public school experiences generally avoid participating in their children's school activities. Having completed college, Lucy knows that she can do most anything, and she fiercely loves her children. Not wanting Bud and Sally to have to fight "generational" teachers who are still at the school, Lucy confronts injustices without fear, taking courageous steps like calling the board of education about the teacher selling Avon.

Lucy's Summary

In the final interview, I asked participants what the qualities of an educated person are, how they felt about their college experience, whether they realized the hopes and dreams that they shared in my classes, and where they saw themselves heading in the future.

> Evaluating my education, I can say that at first coming to college was [for me] to be trained for a job. After I got into it, it got to be more for me, to make me feel better about ME, to increase my self-esteem. I learned a lot. I feel strongly that I am educated as far as book knowledge goes, but I have always considered myself a worldly-wise person as far as common knowledge goes. I believe that being from a large family, you learn so much about different people as

far as attitudes and things. There's always something happening to one of them so that you learn more about common sense. One-on-one common sense is a lot better here in this region because I think that's what helps you through life. And raised in an area like this, you learn to provide for yourself as far as gardening, knowing even out in the wilderness what greens to eat, what roots, where to find shelter and stuff. I can survive. I can cook on an open fire, I am able to can produce, and I can garden.

I believe that everybody gets an education for different reasons. Some do it because they're bored; some do it in order to get a job or just to better themselves. Going to college helped me personally to really find myself, and it even helped in raising my children. It gave me a better outlook on education because I was one of those slackers in high school. And I would love it—it would thrill me to death to go back to Day One and start over again. I tell my son that there are no second chances, so get it right the first time or you go on and try the next time. I have influenced my siblings, though they won't admit it. I was the first of all of us to graduate from high school, and then I graduated from college! Since then, two brothers and two sisters got their GEDs, and one sister went on to nurse's aide training. So I have improved myself and influenced others around me. And I wouldn't trade any of that for what I had before. When I think about where I'll be in ten years, it all depends on Sally's health and my own. In the meantime, I have started the ball rolling; I offered to teach the ladies circle at my church how to decorate cakes, and I hope to get a craft class going as well. I am going to do what I can to make my children's lives good and dedicate my life to making others' lives better as well.

Lessons

Since the beginning of this research, I have admired Lucy because of the odds she overcame to attend Preston College. She has taught me as a teacher to make more of an effort to listen and discern student needs, not to become so involved in completing the syllabus and deadlines, and to be more patient when life circumstances do intervene in students' lives. Working-class students frequently do not have support from home, work full- or part-time jobs to be able to get through college, become overburdened with student loans, and are often overlooked by faculty interested in students' completing their courses in lockstep fashion. Lucy's narrative awoke me to the importance of listening to the silences of all the students in my classroom, male and female, paying more attention to their public and private selves, and making referrals where necessary. I have learned from a colleague recently that he keeps the phone numbers of spouse abuse shelters because he knows how destructive some marriage partners can be when their spouses decide to attend college. I need to be aware of this potential outcome of literacy and be ready to support students in their goals of finishing college.

Although most liberal arts colleges believe that they are educating the whole person, the realistic hope is that education leads to a job with a living wage to make life better for students. Lucy taught me that a college education does not have to lead to employment, another middle-class value assumption. Not completely healthy herself and caring for a sick child, Lucy was unable to work full time, but she used her literacy to manage her children and her life as a single mom. In her life, "literacy is only one factor in complex social and economic interrelationships" (Merrifield et al. 86). Her art, sewing, poetry writing, letters to the editor, and activities with her children provide an alternative definition of an educated person. Though she had to depend on government assistance for her living, Lucy was not selfish; she shared her talents by being involved actively in her son's school and with her church, friends, and family. She helped those in need. Finally, the implication for educators is that Lucy's life is as much a success story as our students who enter the corporate world. She is a good mother and a good citizen in our democracy. Our role, then, is to prepare critical thinkers and problem solvers to contribute those skills for survival in their communities.

The feeling of self-worth that Lucy did not have when she went to college or when she was in her bad marriage finally came from her persistence in pursuing the college degree. Literacy helped her to think more deeply and conceptually and to see that she could put her story into her art and her writing. She was a talented and versatile woman before college, but college magnified the influence of her voice so that the community could hear her whistlin' and crowin'. (See table 3 for a summary of Lucy's post-college literacy practices.)

Table 3. Post-college Literacy Practices: Lucy

Work	Does not work outside her home.
Home	*Reading: Soap Opera Digest, Reader's Digest, Barney Magazine,* Dr. Seuss books, crossword puzzles, swing-set instructions, Bible, recipes, homework, *Cystic Fibrosis Instruction Manual.* Visits bookstores for children.
	Materials: College texts, children's books, yearbooks, videos
	Writing: Pays household bills, records events on calendar, saves medical receipts, keeps a journal of special events and a journal for child with cystic fibrosis, writes personal letters, letters to the editor, and poems (published and unpublished).
	Local expertise: Knowledge of social system to help self and others
	Technology: Phone, microwave, satellite dish

4 / The Literacy Practices of Jean
Learning for Life

When I ran across Jean's name on old class lists, I instantly recalled her essay that ended up in *Voices from the Hill* on the process of making chocolate gravy (see appendix E), a recipe I had never heard of and which ended up in my husband's Appalachian cookbook. Jean graduated with her associate's degree in nursing from Preston College in 1997, three and a half years after she had enrolled. Interviewing her in the nurses' locker room at the end of her twelve-hour shift, I found she exhibited the same spunk and persistence that she had demonstrated when she was enrolled in my class. The major lesson I learned from interviews with Jean and her daughter, Shannon, and from on-the-job shadowing was the importance of lifelong learning for women after college. Managing academic skills and its attendant success had given Jean the desire for learning for the rest of her life so that she had, since college, enrolled in as many continuing education classes as she could and was working to complete her master's in critical care nursing. Below, Jean relates her literacy story, daughter Shannon intersperses comments, and I weave my observations throughout.

> I am Jean. I am short and stocky, full of spunk and energy, and I have sandy-colored hair. Life is good for me, and if it isn't, I try to make it so. At Preston College, I majored in nursing and graduated after three and a half years with a 2.9 average.
>
> My parents are Scotch-Irish, having settled in the region as far back as we can remember. We have lived in the same holler all that time. Neither of my parents completed high school, and, though my mother made it to eighth grade, my

father only made it to early elementary school. I am the middle of three girls, and Mommy wanted all of us to go to college. All three of us have degrees now, and who could have imagined that? One of my sisters is a social worker, the other is a teacher, and I am a nurse. My two sisters, older and younger, were attending college at the same time I was; my younger sister was beginning college, and my older sister was getting her master's in social work.

My husband is disabled but is one of the most caring men I know. He regularly fixes meals, gets my youngest son off to high school, and picks me up from work so that I don't have to drive after working so long. I have three children, two who have graduated from high school and one who is a junior in high school. My older son is a construction worker who has enrolled in technical school but who says that going to school is just too tough. My daughter, Shannon, just graduated from vocational school with her Licensed Practical Nursing [LPN] degree, finishing in the top of her class. I didn't want her to go right into Preston College because I saw so many young people wasting their time and money not studying and not working, and I didn't want her to do the same. Now that she has proven herself, I am encouraging her to attend PC. My son in high school is showing no interest in college, which discourages me. All of my children are like me; they learn from practical activities.

Pre-college Literacy

In our interview, Jean related her family and school literacy history.

My mother and sisters were always reading books, and I always envied them that, but I was a more hands-on person, doing crafts and things with my hands. I read just enough to get by. School was hard, and I found it hard to focus, so I quit school to get married. Except for one English teacher who recognized every individual student and who didn't look down on me, my teachers didn't care about whether they made the material interesting for me because they looked at teaching as a job rather than a vocation. You take a child like me who is not interested in school and put her with a teacher who doesn't care, and then she will never be interested. I left school in the tenth grade and never looked back for twenty years.

In our family, I was the cook and the cleaner and everything. When my husband worked in the mines, he never had to do anything. I always did everything at the house. We'd work outside together some, but inside the house, he never did anything. When he worked in the mines, I'd get up every morning. I'd have his breakfast ready, I'd have his lunch bucket packed, I'd have his clothes laid out, and I'd have everything ready. So all he'd do was just get up and put his clothes on and go to work. And then when he'd come home, I'd have his supper waiting on him and his clothes ready to take a bath and everything. And that's the way it was for almost twenty years. Taking care of him and the children, I did not have much time for many other activities.

After my children came along, I read stories to them and helped them with their homework but regret looking back that I didn't take reading to them more seriously. When I read to my children, we did it for fun. We did it when we'd have time on our hands. But I think now that it needs to be worked into children's system so that it becomes second nature to them. If they have a stronger background in reading, it's a lot easier for them. I intend to read diligently to my grandchildren when they come along, so they will hopefully have an easier time in school and go further than my children or I did. I believe a foundation of reading will help children stay in school, be successful, and want more education after high school.

The next part of my literacy development occurred eighteen years after I dropped out of high school when I decided to take the GED just for fun. One of my friends wanted to take it, and she talked me into going with her, so I really didn't put everything I had into it. I just took it. Well, then I got the results back, and much to my surprise, I passed it; in fact, I did really well.

All of this happened about the time my husband, James, developed black lung disease from working in the mines for so many years and had to quit work. My children were teens and old enough to take care of themselves, and because their dad couldn't work, that gave me the opportunity and incentive to go back to college. I said, "Well, I'll just start from scratch," and that's what I did. And I really liked it because it was better for me in the long run.

After the GED, I applied first for the hospital's respiratory therapy program, which turned me down. Though I was disappointed, it turned out to be a blessing since nursing offered more opportunities than respiratory therapy. I knew from the beginning that I wanted to be a nurse because of growing up close to my grandmother. I loved taking care of her; I just always liked to help. Two years elapsed before I pursued the Preston College nursing program and took the ACT. My first score was 18, but I eventually raised it to the 20 I needed to get in. After I completed my pre-nursing classes, I began to achieve my goal of becoming a nurse.

After getting to know Jean, I imagined her as the child who frightened her friends with snakes and frogs. Compared to her sisters, Jean was the child who could not sit still and was involved in projects. Her public school experience, like many of the other eight women, was not impressive, but when I asked her what the teachers were like, she said that they just did not seem to care for students like her. When I asked why she did not go back to school after she was married, she said that school held no interest.

Most indicative of Jean's spirit is the description of taking the GED on a lark. She had no particular reason for doing it, but the outside verification of not only passing the GED but also doing well on the test without even studying energized Jean. Like many women who spend their time keeping house and raising children, experiencing academic success creates a confirmation of an intellect that raising children does not. Her story reminded me of the women in Philadelphia and North Carolina who spoke of their adult education outside of the traditional public school system offering them the chance to be somebody and to achieve recognition and transformation "in a society where some people count more than others" (Luttrell xv). Staying home and raising a family has no economic recompense, and society in general and some women in the early feminist movement in particular looked down on women who chose that vocation.

College Literacy

Because of her previous public school background and because she had waited twenty years to enter college, Jean's journey from GED to RN was a difficult one. She worked hard to get into the nursing program by spending time while she was taking pre-nursing courses hoping to get an acceptable score on the ACT. Below Jean shares her narrative about her college literacy.

Since I dropped out in tenth grade and did not have time raising a family to do any reading and writing, I had some adjustment to college. Coming back was just like starting school over again. But you can take anybody that's willing to learn and teach her anything, and if you take one twenty years later, and she knows nothing about a particular subject matter, if she wants to, she'll learn. It just takes the will to! Since I did not like reading or writing, I generally learned better if the subject were demonstrated, and I could do it hands-on, like many of my nursing courses.

In composition class, I had a hard time. I didn't know what words to put where or how to express what I wanted to say. But I can say that in your class, I learned how to express myself, mainly how to put a story together with the introduction, the body, and the conclusion. I caught on quickly, and one of my essays, "Grandma's Chocolate Gravy," was even published in *Voices from the Hill.*

The class final was a proficiency exam, which I failed twice. I was devastated, but failing made me more determined to do better the next time. After awhile as I reflected on failing, it was not as bad as I had thought since, in my opinion, the test wasn't an adequate measure of my ability. I had a B in the class going into the exam. What helped me deal with the failure was that I knew one girl in the class who didn't care that much for the class, who goofed off most of the time, and who didn't make good grades. But when she passed the proficiency, I said, "No, no, it doesn't measure what it's supposed to," so I re-enrolled for the class the following semester, passed the proficiency, and received a B for the class.

Another adjustment I had to overcome academically was writing for my nursing classes. On one assignment, I received help from a relative. When I got the assignment back all marked in red, I had a conference with my teacher who encouraged me to learn to trust myself and to avoid amateur advice. When I put what *I did* on the paper, there weren't half as many red marks. I mean, you can take all the pointers and help you can get, but you really have to do it your own way. My teacher helped me see that.

Since reading was hard for me, I tried to find a method to tackle the material. Before the class lesson, usually on the night before, I would read over the material several times. Then, in class it would sink in because the instructor would give demonstrations, and I knew what she was talking about, which helped me understand it better. To fully understand the material in my other classes, I had to find my own way of learning, my own technique of how to handle it, because I know some of the other students would just read the book, and that's all it took. Some would tape the lectures and then listen, and that's how they learned, but that just didn't work for me.

Jean summarizes her life philosophy and key to success in anything she does when she says, "It just takes the will to!" She struggled in my class but turned out essays like the one I submitted to *Voices from the Hill*. In her essay, Jean explained the process of making chocolate gravy to an imagined audience, Allie, the ten-year-old daughter of weekend guests for whom she was trying to fix breakfast, using dialogue throughout. Below is an excerpt.

> "Allie," I said; "I still remember the conversation my grandmother and I would have every morning. My grandmother would walk into the bedroom and say, 'Jean, it is time to get up. Come and eat your breakfast. I have to go milk the cow.' I would reply in a low voice, 'Not right now; I want to sleep just a little bit longer.' Then as she turned to go out of the bedroom, she would say, 'I made chocolate gravy. You'd better get it while it's hot.' Those were the magic words—'CHOCOLATE GRAVY'. Before she got to the kitchen, I was right behind her."
>
> "Sometimes I would get to sit and watch my grandma go through the steps to make chocolate gravy. She would use these ingredients: 1 ½ cups sugar, 4 tablespoons flour, 4 tablespoons cocoa, ½ cup milk. First, she would combine the sugar, flour, and cocoa in a bowl, making sure they were all mixed together. Then, she would pour the dry ingredients into a cooker on the stove. Next, Grandma would add the milk and water, stirring until thoroughly mixed. She placed the cooker on medium heat until it started to boil. Grandma would stir the mixture until it was just right, making sure not to let it scorch." (appendix E)

Jean shows control of dialogue, which adds interest to the process that by itself might have sounded too much like a cookbook recipe, and has a good sense of audience. For women who were in traditional roles in their families, cooking and raising children often became topics for essays.

Jean's observation about the proficiency exam points to the difficulty of using these kinds of exams as the final in first-semester composition classes. Students write responses to a choice of prompts in this two-hour exam. As their instructor, I grade the exam first, then another English faculty member grades it blindly. Should there be a disagreement between the original two, another professor will resolve the dilemma. Students who fail have a chance to re-take the exam before the next semester starts. If they fail again, as Jean did, then they re-enroll in English 111. If students pass the exam, then the instructor averages the grades together and adds the score to the semester grade. This exam creates a great deal of anxiety because even if students have decent grades going into the exam, they cannot pass the class without passing the proficiency. Though the college's rationale is to ensure that students enrolling in the more difficult second part of the composition class will be successful in writing the more traditional research paper, the exam has problems. With a two-hour writing prompt, students may experience many kinds of interference. They might not find a topic that inspires them; they may be too nervous in a timed situation; other factors may intervene to make it a bad day; or the finished product may not be typical of their semester work. Mainly the proficiency acts in a gatekeeper function, and the teacher ends up teaching to the test and arming students to pass through faculty who might grade it differently than he or she does. In Jean's example, a weak, lazy student got lucky and passed while Jean failed. Though she benefited from another semester in English to compensate for her weak English background, Jean pointed to some valid shortcomings of the system.

The amount of reading required in Jean's pre-nursing and nursing classes interested me since she had shared how much she hated reading. To prepare herself, she read the text thoroughly the night before and had the material reinforced with the instructor's lecture and demonstration. Later, she would demonstrate that same behavior when she worked on her nursing shift. In writing assignments, she learned to trust herself and not rely on outside help, and she also learned to work with the instructor to achieve her goals.

Next, I wanted to find out how going back to college affected her family since she had described such traditional roles for herself. Jean and her daughter, Shannon, help me illustrate the effect of college literacy on families.

How did all of this affect my family? I tried not to let my studies interrupt my family's schedule too much. I turned on my light that clamps on to the bed every night after I got all the kids tucked away, the house cleaned, and that's when I did my studying and reading when it was the quietest. Often I had that light on until one or two in the morning.

As a family, we'd still visit places that we liked to, but now I carried my books with me. We would even sometimes just go to the grocery store at Preston, but my books went too. When we went on vacation to North Carolina, my books went too. If I got a spare moment, I read. I even took my books to football games and other places so that I could read while I sat in the bleachers.

Shannon, my twenty-year-old daughter, can tell you about how she reacted to my coming to college:

My mother had been at home for fourteen years as the mother—supper every evening at 3 o'clock and there all the time when you needed her. When Mom went back to college, my dad, my two brothers, and I had to pull together and support her by taking on responsibilities as far as washing dishes, doing laundry, sweeping, mopping, fixing supper, and helping each other. The adjustment was difficult, but everyone worked together, including my older and younger brothers who were used to being waited on. We came first, and she did her studying at bedtime.

While we were growing up, my mother read books, newspapers, and magazines and wrote letters to family in Ohio. I was in high school when Mom went to college, so she helped me with my high school writing, especially how to put an essay together and to know where the parts of an essay go.

From the start of college to the finish, I noticed that Mom always worked hard and never let anything bring her down, and now she's got a lot of self-confidence. She's a lot more determined. And I think that she will continue to go back for more education. There's no obstacle too big for her! My mother took the step to go back to college in the face of people like my dad's parents who said that my mom should stay at home, but she let them know: "This is what I want, and this is what I'm going to do, and I'm going to make it regardless." My mother has given me that confidence. She was my role model for finishing the Licensed Practical Nursing program through the vocational school. I am proud of my mother. Mom has definitely affected my life.

Jean continues:

Yes, my immediate family was one hundred percent behind me. My husband began helping me with my chores and has taken them over now since I work the night shift. He would help me with my tests even though he only had an eighth grade education himself. He never, not one time, asked me not to, let alone told me not to, finish college.

His parents, my in-laws, did not feel the same. His family is more like prehistoric age, and they felt that I should be home doing cooking, cleaning, and caring for the children. My own parents encouraged me; my mother didn't go back to school or anything. She just had the family. And that's what kind of sometimes amazes me where I graduated high school and then my father didn't even finish, and so we had no model of college growing up, but still they produced three girls, and every one of them has got a degree.

Although Shannon went to LPN school, I cannot get my sons interested in further schooling. Like me, they tend to be hands-on learners. My older son went to the local vocational school and didn't feel challenged enough, so he quit and is working construction. He hopes to go back to school when he can save up enough money for it. My younger son, a junior in high school, has to be forced to do his homework. He wants to go to vocational school when he graduates. School has never been his thing. I don't know whether it was challenging enough for him or what.

Mother and daughter show what can happen when families pull together. Jean's return to college turned the family upside down, but all worked to make it easier for this to happen. This scenario repeated itself in many of the other families. Judith said that her girls would announce, "Mom's got a test tomorrow; let's let her study!" Like the other women, Jean put her children's work first and then spent the late evenings doing her own work, but she also took her books wherever the children were, using her time well. Mainly Jean set an example for her children, especially her daughter, of finishing college and of achieving goals. In her LPN program, Shannon had some of the same nursing texts her mother had used in the Preston College program, so they could share notes. Not surprisingly, Shannon graduated tops in her class. Though frustrated about her sons, Jean seemed to credit their lack of interest in college to their being more experiential learners.

Because of her determination, Jean dealt with the negative reaction of her "prehistoric" in-laws and successfully completed her associate's degree in nursing. She graduated in May 1997 and was hired at the local hospital in July 1997.

Post-college Literacy

Jean worked the 7 P.M. to 7 A.M. shift in the Medical Intensive Care Unit (MICU), so I decided to spend the first four hours of that shift observing her reading and writing on the job. The information below resulted from my time there and one follow-up interview. Observing Jean's work greatly impressed me and taught me more than any textual description about the importance of workplace literacy. She narrates her story below.

Workplace Literacy: Writing

The nursing program at Preston College definitely prepared me for the skills I have used at the hospital, but I was scared to death once I actually started working. It takes awhile to gain confidence, just as it took me awhile to adjust to college. As a nurse, knowing how to read and write is crucial to being successful. I would say that 50 percent or more of my day is taken up with writing nursing assessment notes about my patients. Because I am too busy taking care of patients, I use shortened phrases and acronyms to facilitate quick but accurate notes. I am never without pen and paper while I work, stuffing both into one of my pockets while I check an IV or perform another nursing procedure. Because the hospital is so understaffed, I have not had a formal orientation to the MICU nursing duties, but I have plunged in, using skills learned in the heart unit and asking for help when I need it.

To prepare myself, I go in forty-five minutes before the shift debriefing. When I get there, I can look in the charts, I get my list of patients, and I pick up any little odds and ends that the previous nurses have indicated. I take notes down and build on them. With my notes in hand and the huge notebook for each patient filled with doctor's orders and nursing assessment forms, I then meet with the nurses from the prior shift as they review each patient's conditions, medicines, behaviors, patient visitors, and other information about the patients in my charge (usually two).

As the shift begins, I add to the paper with the notes taken from before the shift began, which I eventually record on the nursing assessment form for as long as the patient remains in the hospital. On this form I record items such as general appearance, mental status, skin, pulmonary status, cardiac status, GI status, bowel sounds, feeding tube, and renal information. In addition to the assessment form, I fill out an extra report form for follow-through for the entire time the patient is in MICU, which records vital signs, hemo dynamic, cardio-pulmonary, neuro, lab, intake, output, and critical care flow sheet. I chart every two hours and attach all of this information to the form, which becomes part of the patient's notebook.

I have my own system for taking notes, my own nursing assessment values. I go from top to bottom of the nursing assessment form, and it's a lot easier. I can write faster once I get my system down pat. As I visit my patients, I continue to add information to the sheet I began taking notes on at the beginning of my shift, and then I transfer the information to the permanent nursing assessment form. The attending physician as well as the nurses that relieve my shift rely on this information.

Workplace Literacy: Reading

With each shift, I also need to check all the medicines (meds) that each of my patients is taking. I read through the doctor's orders in a huge red notebook, and as I check, I initial next to the med, which shows the next nurse that I was aware of meds and the exact amount indicated. I check as far back as the patient has been in ICU. In each room, I check the patient's heart monitor, check the various intravenous fluids going into his or her body, and read the computerized monitors. I also have to be able to read results that come back from various laboratory tests. For example, an arterial blood graph would show whether patients need more oxygen or have their oxygen turned down if they're getting too much. I consult the *Nurses IV Drug Handbook* to check on the medicines for one patient to be sure of the medicine's compatibility with the fluids going into the patient's system. I also consult the computer to check on availability of medicines for each dosage during my shift so that I can get what I need from the pharmacy before it closes from midnight to 7 A.M. If I need something like a bag of fluid for one patient, I key it in to the computer, which has every patient's medicines listed, check what I need, and call to ask if the pharmacy can send it up right away. I check blood levels because antibiotics can get toxic. All of the information I record goes in the notebook, which follows the patient wherever he or she goes in case the patient is transferred to another floor.

What stood out for me when I was observing Jean's literacy was the small scrap of paper on which she recorded her preliminary notes and how she built on it with other information she listed above that would be transferred to the nursing assessment form. Her preparation for the night shift reminded me of her system for tackling academic reading and writing. The information she gathered from reading the notes ahead was confirmed by what she heard from the prior shift's nurses, just as the college instructor's demonstration or lecture confirmed the reading she had done the night before. Whether it arose from her overzealous nature to do a good job or insecurity about not doing an adequate job since she was so new in the MICU, Jean wanted to be able to do the best for her patients.

The night of my observation, Jean was assigned two patients, a fifty-two-year-old woman dying of heart failure and an eighty-two-year-old man in isolation because of his resistance to an antibiotic. The patient in isolation was there because there had been no other beds in the hospital, but when one became available, Jean began his transfer to another floor. Before they moved him, she had to transfer the notes from her scrap of paper to the nursing assessment form. She recorded, "awake, arouses easily, and talks incoherently at times." She observed wound dressings, medicines he was taking, the site injury (hip replacement), the color of his urine in the catheter, and other items. As required, she signed her name after each time entry. Occasionally, she recorded, "no change noted," "linens changed," "no distress noted," or "isolation precautions in use." Additionally, she recorded what the position of the bedside rails was, whether the call bell was within reach, what the heart rhythm was, when meds were given, and finally, "will continue to assess for further needs." For his transfer, she added the name of the nurse she had talked to on the floor where he was being transferred, the name of the charge nurse on her floor, and the name of the doctor who authorized the transfer. The other patient in her care that night was dying, and the family had requested that the medical staff withdraw her life support systems at midnight. Jean received specific instructions from the woman's attending physician on how to perform the procedure. The patient died early the next morning.

One of the nurses on duty with Jean made the most pointed comment about the importance of the nursing notes. She sometimes felt that they were writing to protect themselves and the hospital from legal problems instead of recording information that would help save lives, though she acknowledges that one mistake by a nurse could cause the patient to suffer or, in the worst-case scenario, die.

I was most impressed with the care, the cooperation, and the hard work of the nurses in the MICU but was disturbed that they did not recognize the importance of their literacy. When I came onto the floor to do this participant observation, the other nurses made me feel welcome, but once they knew I was Jean's former English teacher (I had actually taught one of the prior shift nurses as well),

I heard all kinds of comments that illustrated their vision of writing teachers as grammar police and writing in college as unrelated to workplace literacy. The charge nurse said that he had always hated writing in school. One nurse noted that "we don't write in complete sentences here"; another added, "Don't check my work!" Workplace literacy is more concrete and less ambiguous than academic literacy, which requires voicing thoughts, feelings, and opinions taboo in nursing notes because of their life and death ramifications (Sitler). Though academic and workplace literacy differ, I was upset that they had a view of their writing as somehow not good enough.

Jean observed during my visit that the college nursing program had adequately prepared her for the reading and writing she had to do as a nurse. Academic writing gave her confidence, but writing as a nurse required a different set of demands and purposes. She was concerned about the accuracy of her notes, but she used her literacy constantly to assure adequate care of her charges and impressed me with her nursing knowledge and empathy.

Career Advancement and Lifelong Learning

Among my three case studies, Jean was the most energetic about continuing her education. She describes below her feelings about becoming a better nurse.

> I want to be the best nurse possible, so I am anxious to learn as much as possible about my job. I was hired at this hospital two months after my graduation in May 1997 as a staff nurse on the midnight shift, and I have been promoted many times. In one of my most recent positions, I was relief charge nurse for heart patients. When the regular charge nurse was off-duty, I made assignments, observed what the other nurses were doing, and made sure everything went smoothly. Then I had extra paperwork to fill out. I looked out for the oncoming shift to make sure they had enough work. In that job, I had learned about heart patients, but I

had gone as far as I could in the learning process. I mean, I could have stayed and would have eventually become charge nurse, but that's not enough for me. It would have been the same thing over and over. I thought there would be challenge in the MICU, and in February 1999, I applied for that position, which I now occupy.

To learn more, I participate in many required, hospital-sponsored continuing education programs and in-service workshops for nurses. To qualify for working in the open-heart surgery unit about to open at the hospital, I began the master's in critical care nursing through a correspondence course from Regency College in New York. In this program, students work at their own pace with the book learning, then they participate in clinicals, and when they are ready, they take their test in Cincinnati or Lexington. When I finish, I will have a master's in nursing, my long-term goal.

In addition to the critical care degree, I have recently taken a certification course for intravenous care nursing. For training, I attended a review class at the local community college where they gave me a list of articles that I can get at the library about different kinds of IV accesses and angiopaths and stuff like that. And then they give you a list of books that you can buy, money out of your pocket. But if you're really dedicated or really want to do it, then you'll buy a couple of books. It takes a lot of studying of signs and symptoms of different diseases, knowing medications and IV solutions for those diseases. The test for the certification is twice a year and has a 60 percent pass rate because of its difficulty. If I successfully pass the exam, I would have the letters "ICRN" placed on my nursing badge along with my RN. I would then keep up my certification with 30 contact hours of classes every two years. For critical care nursing certification, I needed 1,700 contact hours, which I have planned to accumulate within the following years by working more hours in the MICU. After that, I earn the designation of CCRN on my badge. Neither of these certifications nor the master's degree guarantees an automatic raise in pay, but they do increase my employability.

What struck me during our interviews was her statement that "that's not enough for me" in terms of her work and job advancement; she wanted to keep improving and moving up. At the time of the interview, she was studying for certification in intravenous nursing, a course that was a combination of classroom and off-site readings and studying. This course was not sponsored directly by the hospital; it supplemented the required continuing education classes for nursing that she attended regularly. Jean was like the parched sojourner in the desert coming to a watering hole, soaking up all the education that she could get.

Jean changed her literacy practices from purely practical to academic when she made the choice to attend college, making sense of her life as she contributed to her family's financial support after her husband was laid off in the mines. I believe that she expanded her definition of herself as a learner and hence found out that something she had thought unattainable became attainable, proving that

> higher education may be particularly significant for adult women as a means of challenging their limiting self-perceptions of themselves as learners, confronting the limitations of previously held beliefs about women's roles, [and] obtaining power and status in the workplace and community. (Hayes and Flannery 76)

Consciously or not, Jean illustrates the principle of continued development that "assumes that literacy, as an inseparable part of the person, must also grow and develop as the adult ages and takes on new challenges in the world" (Neilsen 9). As her daughter, Shannon, stated in her interview, nothing can stop her mother now.

Home Literacy

Since it was not part of my methodology to visit Jean's home, I asked her to describe her literacy activities at home and learned that her energy level never appears to drop as she pursues reading and writing for her continuing education courses and for home crafts and building.

> Because of my job, I have to do all of my studying for continuing education classes at home. My method of studying for these certifications is to try to understand the material I read; I develop flash cards to study. After reading the material, I take copious notes and summarize relevant details on a 5 x 8 index card and quiz myself with the flash cards. I highlight in yellow the information I want to remember.

> So I do a majority of writing at home because I'm studying. I would say that I do more writing than I did in college. If we get a patient on the floor with something we don't know or haven't heard of, I'll go home, and I'll read up on it. I'll drag my old medical books out and look through and see what I can find. And if the lab values are wrong or somebody's got something out of whack, I go back, and I just try to figure out why and read about it. In addition to studying my test material, I read my nursing texts and nursing journals like *RN* and *American Journal of*

Nursing regularly at home. Using the Internet, I look for information on new medication, new techniques, new illnesses, old illnesses, or anything to do with nursing.

Since my night shift is generally twelve hours, I don't have much time for community activities. After I sleep during the day, my husband fixes my supper, and I am off again to work. He's a jewel. He cleans house. He helps do the laundry. He'll have the whole supper fixed when I get home from work, and he cooks a big meal. Any spare time I have, I spend it at home studying for exams or doing handicrafts for relaxation.

I still feel that I am not a good reader because, unlike my mother and sister, I do not read books like Harlequin romances or Stephen King. Mother is still a really good reader. They all are. I'm the oddball. I might pick up more reading if I had more leisure time. If I do keep up with anything, it has to do with nursing.

I also like physical work. My husband and I began our married life making payments on and living in a trailer. When we sold the trailer, we built our first house, then another two-story house. We built it. It's ours. We built it with our hands, and we owe nothing on it. When I was nervous while studying for my nursing boards, my husband and I built a gazebo over our creek bed. Knowing how hard it would be for my husband after he was declared disabled to sit around while I was working, I borrowed money to get a 1951 Chevrolet for him to rebuild.

I like to learn, and I know that reading is a big, important thing, but most of my work is creative hands-on stuff like quilting, embroidering, and helping my husband build outside furniture. We subscribe to the local paper, and we own a set of encyclopedias and handicraft books.

Once again, Jean has a method for studying—which includes reading and writing—that helps her to make sense of dense medical terminology. She uses flash cards (see figure 3) to make sense of the material she needs to review for a test. I believe that her college experience directly influenced her methods because they so closely parallel the way she handled learning in college. She added to her core medical knowledge about particular questions that work-related problems created by consulting her college nursing texts, nursing journals, or medical sites on the Internet.

What cries out to me is her continued definition of herself as a poor reader when she reads nursing journals, the Internet, and complex medical books well enough to pass certification exams. Like Lucy, Jean cannot believe that she is a good reader because of her narrow definition of reading as relating only to novels when, in fact, many would see her choice of reading medical tomes over Harlequin romances a superior one. Apparently, the only real writing occurs in the classroom; the only real reading occurs when reading Shakespeare. The obvious differences between job and college writing are real, but readers such as Jean should not be self-disparaging. Our educational system needs to re-think the attitude it conveys that makes Jean describe herself as the oddball in a reading family despite the hours she spends reading and writing on her job and at home.

Most interesting to me was the role reversal in her marriage. From her detailed description earlier of all that she did for James when he worked in the mines to her description above of all the work he was doing for her while she worked in the hospital, I got a clear picture of a supportive husband comfortable with his new role—a dramatic contrast to Lucy's husband, Matt, who not only did not support her but who in fact abused her.

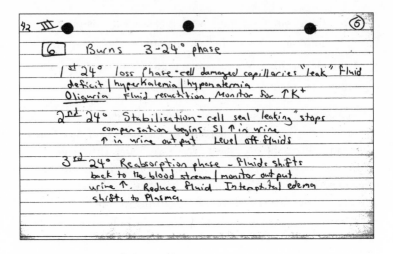

6 Burns 3-24° phase

1st 24° loss phase - cell damaged capillaries "leak" Fluid
deficit / hyperkalemia / hyponatremia
Oliguria Fluid resuscitation, Monitor for ↑K+

2nd 24° Stabilization - cell seal "leaking" stops
compensation begins Sl ↑ in urine
↑ in urine output Level off fluids

3rd 24° Reabsorption phase - Fluids shifts
back to the blood stream / monitor output
urine ↑. Reduce Fluid Interophital edema
shifts to Plasma.

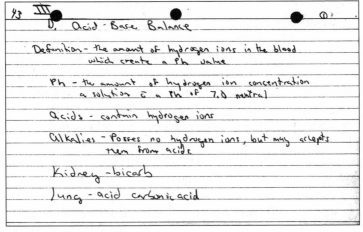

D. Acid - Base Balance

Definition - the amount of hydrogen ions in the blood
which create a Ph value

Ph - the amount of hydrogen ion concentration
a solution c̄ a Ph of 7.0 neutral)

Acids - contain hydrogen ions

Alkalies - Posses no hydrogen ions, but may accepts
them from acids.

Kidney - bicarb

Lung - acid carbonic acid

Fig. 3. Jean's flash cards for studying

Jean's Summary

College has made me and my family more financially secure. Even with the threat of a nursing strike, I feel with my nursing degree that if I wanted to move to another place, I think I could find a job somewhere else. It might take a little while, but I think I could find one. During college we had to rely on my husband's disability check and my financial aid loans; now we are looking to buy a retirement place in Tennessee to fish and farm. I'll probably keep working so we'll have enough money so we can retire and do what we want to.

Mainly, my nursing education gave my something that nobody can take away from me. I have more self-confidence after college with the knowledge that I'm just as good as anybody but no better. I was proud that I graduated from Preston College's nursing program, which has the reputation for being hard compared to other nursing programs in the region. Nurses who graduate from Preston College end up with jobs at the local hospital, and they're still working there. Looking back at my college experience, I think going back to school and seeing so many young ones learning gave me the idea of seeing where my strengths were, because I saw how many did not make it and how many thought it was just fun and then they realized they had lost it all.

What inspires me most is setting an example for my children and then knowing that I've got a story to tell my grandchildren. And that can always help. I think I will be a strong influence on them, especially, like I said, the reading of books. I know that I'll make a difference, and that little difference, to me, will be worthwhile. Better than running for president. Besides the legacy I leave my children, I hope that my grandchildren will not, if I have anything to say about it, drop out of school as I did. And they will love reading more than I did.

I believe that an educated person is someone who doesn't think that she knows it all and always has something to learn. Even with nursing skills, I feel that I don't know it all; I just know a little bit. But if you know that, and you're willing to work for it, you'll learn. The college experience allowed me to express myself, gave me the skills for my nursing career, and now I am ready to keep learning for the rest of my life. I have the confidence now to do more than I ever thought possible because of college. I will keep learning as long as I have breath in me.

Lessons

Educators tell us that generally success in college depends on social class "origins [which] are more powerful in determining success" than academic or other factors (Knox, Lindsay, and Kolb 13). Those social class origins "have more to do with benefits of literacy" than the promises of literacy acquisition (Street, *Literacy in Theory* 84). So, in many ways, Jean was the least likely of the three participants to be in college in terms of her parents' lack of formal education, her own incomplete secondary education, and her traditional cultural role as wife and mother. She was certainly the least likely to have gone on to pursue all the continuing education programs that she was pursuing at the time of the study. She was still insecure about the way she sounded, evidenced by the numerous changes she made to her transcript (which was already slightly edited); she said she did not want to sound like a "hillbilly."

What Jean taught me is that I need to watch out for my attitude to weaker students, especially those like Jean who dropped out of high school. Determination and motivation have as much to do with academic success as any other educational factor, and I need to provide opportunities and support services like tutoring for those who want education so badly but are ill-prepared to be successful. Overlooking these kinds of students because their backgrounds are so weak keeps them powerless.

Jean's inspirational behavior reminded me of my mother's constant thirst for more learning once she had taken one continuing education course and my own hunger for more education. Learning satisfies the heart-hunger for esteem and offers the chance to build on talents and abilities, to expand the mind, and ultimately to complete the task of achieving a college degree, something highly valued in our society (Knox, Lindsay, and Kolb 173). Jean ultimately is whistlin' and crowin' and coming to good ends. (See table 4 for Jean's post-college literacy practices.)

Table 4. Post-college Literacy Practices: Jean

Work	*Reading:* Charts, doctor's orders, lab tests, drug handbooks
	Writing: Makes notes throughout shift, records information on nursing assessment forms, initials notes and changes, writes in patient notebooks.
	Technology: Checks patient pharmacy records, orders medicines.
	Job advancement: Studying for the following certifications: IVRN, ICRN, CCRN.
Home	*Reading:* House plans, handicraft books, encyclopedias, *RN* and *American Journal of Nursing,* college nursing texts, triweekly newspaper, flash cards and study guides for advanced certifications. Prefers working with hands to reading novels.
	Writing: Takes notes for test purposes, highlighting for emphasis.
	Technology: Uses Internet at home to look up diseases and medicines for patients.

5 / The Literacy Practices of Sarah
Fulfilling a Mother's Dream

When I remember Sarah, I recall a perfect student who worked hard to achieve the highest level possible in my class. Serious and focused then, Sarah made the same impression in the first interview that took place in the counseling center office where she worked. Her focus at the time was raising her sixteen-year-old son by herself and doing the best job possible as a foster care worker. Because Sarah spoke constantly of the effect her mother, Naomi, had on her getting a college education, I wanted to interview Naomi and had that good fortune after I had chosen Sarah for the case studies. Sarah and Naomi taught me about the intergenerational nature of literacy.

> I am Sarah. Blond and pert, I am an "in-charge," no-nonsense person. I am the single mother of Luke, a high schooler who just got his driver's license, a kid who has grown up with me through the divorce from his father and my second marriage and then divorce; he is someone who has made the sacrifice all the more important.
>
> The key person in my development, especially with regard to education, is my mother, Naomi, whose dream of my graduating from college was realized when I walked across the stage in 1993. I have vague memories of my dad who treated me like a princess but who died in the mines when I was five. I admire my mother for raising me single-handedly on the disability check she received from social

security. Mother could easily have a college degree; she reads so extensively, especially about the Bible.

I graduated from Preston College with a psychology/human services major, and I got a job with the major mental health provider in the region three months after I began applying for jobs. Now I am a case manager for a private religious organization which works with severely abused foster children. Because of this grueling work, I like my solitude in the evening, and when I have time, I like to go fishing for escape and recreation.

Pre-college Literacy

As part of this research, I interviewed Sarah's mother, Naomi. In our first interview, Sarah constantly mentioned her mother in the conversation: her mother's emphasis on education, her mother bringing home stacks of books from the library, her mother challenging her preacher on biblical truths, and so on. She said, "My mom push[ed] me to have something better than what she had—a very limited education, limited abilities. I guess ever since I was little I can remember her going over and over how important education was" (January 25, 1999). So I was happy to travel about forty minutes from Preston and down a mountain holler to interview Naomi, who combined intellect and common sense much like her daughter. Though at one point Naomi described herself as uneducated, since she had only finished eighth grade, later in the interview she labeled herself as a "flat-out good student" when she had been in school. For three hours, I listened to Naomi's remarkable literacy history, and I thought she could speak for herself about the importance of Sarah's pre-college literacy.

When Sarah was five years old, her father, a bolt machine operator, was electrocuted in the mines. Do you know what it's like to have someone knock on your door and tell you your husband is dead? I was left bereft of the breadwinner in our family, I had no skills to market myself, and Sarah was left without a father. I wanted her to be more prepared than I was for such an event, so I always taught Sarah to stand on her own two feet, never to be left like I was. If she got an education, she wouldn't have to depend on any man. In fact, I remained single until Sarah was in high school: I would allow no men near the house while she was a child. I remarried after Sarah left home.

What kept me from completing high school is a story in itself. In the 1950s, the Preston County school system required students to buy all the books for high school, a huge expense for my family. When my older sister quit high school to get married after my parents had sacrificed to buy her books, they got angry and would not let me go. That did not stop me from reading. Growing up, I'd read all kinds of books, like those true story books—but they all began sounding like soap operas. I learned also that common sense will teach you things if you'll use what the good Lord has given you. I see people that are really educated that don't have the common sense to cross the road.

With a social security check of about $48 a month, I eked out a living for us, sacrificing so that Sarah had everything she needed. I never drew a welfare check in my life! When Sarah was in high school, I finally took a job driving a school bus to help with expenses. Every chance I had, I put away money for Sarah's college fund, which amounted to $10,000 when she graduated from high school. When Sarah ran away to get married, it broke my heart, but I convinced her to complete high school.

Sarah and I traveled regularly to the public library in the nearby town about thirty minutes away because the elementary and high school libraries at Sarah's school were so limited. Even now, my second husband and I spend time at this library and bring home huge quantities of books.

Many of the books I check out are biblical commentaries, which help me in reading the Bible. I try to get as involved as possible in my reading, and I can read for hours at a time. I prefer the New to the Old Testament because it shows us how to conduct ourselves, how to apply the words to our daily lives, and how to make us better persons. And it will point out when you're not a better person.

My method of reading is simple. I come to so many words that I don't understand because I don't have much of an education. If I go on and read a little bit farther, and it still doesn't make that much sense to me, I'll back up and say, "Well, maybe I'm not understanding this word," and I look it up, which puts a whole different light or meaning on Bible verses. In contrast, the preacher at the Pentecostal church where I attend approaches the Bible differently. He has a very closed mind, which is the result of a lack of education. With education comes more understanding. I want to hoard everything I can about the Bible, and he is trapped within his mind. Though he is a good man, he doesn't pronounce the words correctly, and words don't mean what he thinks they mean. He won't go back, and he won't look the words up, so I try to bring some of this to his attention, and he gets upset with me and says, "I am the pastor." I don't believe that his authority is based on the accurate interpretation of the word.

In fact, I have learned from my reading about various interpretations of biblical passages. For example, King James had the Bible interpreted, according to one writer I read, seven times before he'd have it released into English, because he wanted the words there as HE wanted it written. And he didn't want too much said about women. For instance, in the book of Romans (I believe it's the sixteenth chapter) where it says "Phoebe the servant." Well, in the real Bible it doesn't say that. It says "Phoebe the deaconess." I mean, that's on the scrolls in Jerusalem. You can hire a rabbi over there to read them, and there's a lot of the Bible that's been changed around. And I learn about these things, and it gives me a better understanding.

I believe that learning goes on throughout your life and that when you get close-minded, then you can never learn.

And I don't care if you live to be a hundred; if you keep an open mind, you can always learn something new. And every woman in the world has a right for an education however pretty or ugly she is. If you are educated, then you can never let other people tell you how to live.

From what we would call humble beginnings, Naomi arose from the ashes like a phoenix. Her parents could not afford to take the chance that they had taken on her sister, so Naomi could not complete her formal education. Her continuous reading and thirst for knowledge is an example to us of informal literacy and self-education and was a model for Sarah as she grew up. She "attempt[s] to make sense of the text . . . get[s] to the meaning by unraveling . . . texts" and recursively constructs meaning of her reading (Goodman 84).

A naturally curious person, Naomi described to me her experiences as a school bus driver. When she would drive a busload of high school students to an activity at Preston College and wait for them to complete their activities, she would roam over to the biology lab and examine the specimens on display. She asked me if I had seen the same specimens and asked if I didn't think they were fascinating. This curiosity coupled with her voracious reading prompted me to suggest to Naomi that she return to college. Though she waved me off as if that were impossible, Sarah believed that her mother could easily be a religion major and probably teach her teachers a thing or two.

Naomi's stalwart determination to do the best she could to make life better for Sarah and her discipline in not going on welfare was impressive. Her close reading of commentaries on the King James Bible was especially revealing to me; her rhetoric sounds strongly feminist, though she—like many of the Preston County women—resisted that label because of its radical connections. More interesting was her observation that no one can tell a person how to live if he or she is educated; people can be manipulated if they are ignorant.

Most impressive were her encounters with her pastor, whom Sarah described as "close-minded." His reactions to Naomi's confrontations spoke of his unwillingness to dialogue with her; she posed a threat because she appeared to be more literate than he was, even if he had finished high school (though some pastors called to the ministry eschew seminary training and may have limited literacy). Her observation that people must keep on learning until they die conveyed to me her commitment to lifelong learning, which had an effect on Sarah.

This encounter with Naomi made me curious about how the other seven women came to college, knowing that education begets education and that "highly educated parents are more likely than their less-educated counterparts to raise children who themselves recognize the value of education" (Pascarella and Terenzini 414). Many parents of the other seven participants dropped out of school or graduated from high school but did not go on to college, but they, like Naomi, wanted better lives for their children, which they thought would be possible with a college education.

In fact, Naomi's belief in the power of education to free Sarah from the economic woes Naomi herself suffered was echoed by mothers of the other participants. Judith's mother encouraged her by saying, "'I didn't get this opportunity because when I grew up, the family was only concerned with the boys. Only the boys got to go on to high school and to college. It's [going to college] just too important not to do'" (February 5, 1999). Hope's mother, a hospital dietitian who died before she saw her daughter graduate, repeated constantly to Hope when she was in high school, "Go to school and be a teacher" (January 20, 1999). After her mother's death, Hope's dad actively supported her and offered financial help for summer school and other educational expenses. These parents support Carolyn Leste Law's observation that parents of working-class children hope that education will help their children realize their dreams, but they want them to "come home . . . essentially the same" (5). Once their daughters made the choice to return to college, the mothers frequently provided meals and cared for their grandchildren while their daughters attended classes. Though none of their daughters chose the traditional path to higher education, the mothers encouraged their daughters to enroll.

Maintaining their roles as the purveyors of education and culture like their mothers, these mountain women placed their families first, like the mothers in the Mothers' Center movements (Belenky, Bond, and Weinstock). Because they were confident about their mothering skills, the Preston County women made sure that their college education did not interfere with their maternal responsibilities. Most waited until their children's homework was completed before they did their own studying, even if it meant staying up later at night. They juggled their obligations with supportive spouses and children in some cases or battled nonsupportive family and/or spouses in others. Gillian Pascall and Roger Cox observe among their working-class informants returning to college that they

> placed education within the context of lives in which responsibility for others, particularly children, was assumed as a priority. To that extent, it could be argued that neither phase [of their education] had undermined traditional values or provided women with a means to escape the duties that go with them. (143)

The low-status Appalachian women in Judith Fiene's research on social services affirm the centrality of their roles as mothers. Being good mothers meant putting children's needs before their own and surmounting "uncommon obstacles" to keep children from harm (51). The same theme echoes in Carol Giesen's study of coal miners' wives: "Homemaking responsibilities were central in the lives of even the several women who had thoughts to more education or training for self-employment" (26).

As much as their mothers wanted education for their daughters, so the participants were hoping that their being in college would influence their children to go to college at the traditional age, after high school. Faith stated that the main reason she returned to finish her degree was to influence her son to finish high school and go on to college (January 26, 1999). Jean felt that "they [the children] have seen that if you don't get it [college education] now, it's a lot harder to get it later" (April 29, 1999). Sarah, like her mother before her, emphasized college to her son, who was a sophomore in high school: "There are times he'll say he's not going to school, but when he's out away from me talking, he's wants to further his education. He's already sent out information for colleges" (January 25, 1999).

Other study participants were frustrated that their children who had completed high school were not enrolling in college. For example, Polly's children had no interest in furthering their education; in fact, one son had dropped out in tenth grade and was driving a coal truck. She was frustrated: "How do you encourage kids? How do you get them to go to college? Because I always wanted mine to, but they just never did" (January 21, 1999). Though Mary's son was offered a Preston College alumni scholarship, he declined the offer in order to work construction. Judith's two older sons had finished high school and were trained by their computer companies to work. Jean's son was working construction; only her daughter had completed an LPN program at the local technical school.

At the time of these interviews in the winter of 1999, only one out of the seven collective children of the participants who had graduated from high school had attended a postsecondary program. Though my purpose did not include fieldwork to determine the reasons for this temporary block in the intergenerational chain of academic literacy, I hypothesize several possibilities. One reason might be that five of the seven children were male and might have looked to their fathers as models, and only one of the fathers had three years of college; in fact, some had dropped out of high school. Since high schoolers are often influenced by their peers, these children could have bypassed college because none of their peers were intending to go. Another reason could be that the children may have seen the sacrifices their mothers had made and decided it was not worth it, much like the participants in Deborah Brandau's literacy study in upstate New York. A colleague who has taught composition in central Appalachia for years has observed that frequently the phenomenon will skip generations, so that these women's grandchildren might attend college (Vanderbrake, personal interview). Some of the children may in fact enroll in college as they get older, just as their mothers did. For the children who were still at home, it was too soon to tell.

In any case, the effects on their children do not end with whether they go to college or not. As Lucy reports, "Going to college helped me personally to really find myself, and it even helped in raising my children" (April 22, 1999). Having the women set the example of finishing what they started influenced many around them, including their children.

The stories told by these women—first-generation college students—about the intergenerational influence on family members is repeated in other literacy studies. First-generation and nontraditional African American women social work majors in a rural Georgia college were influenced by their grandmothers and older brothers to enroll in college, refuting the argument that single-parented, "absent-father" homes are weak. Like the Preston County women, no one in that study mentioned inspirational teachers, since most had had poor public school experiences (Hammons-Bryner). In Marcia Egan's study of social work, pre-med, and counseling graduate students who grew up in rural Appalachia, it was fathers and grandfathers who influenced the women to enroll in college.

The dream of a better life for working-class families does not always pan out, and social mobility as we know it does not always happen. In fact, "the promise that all Americans can move up the socioeconomic ladder if they work hard enough—is not a reality," a concept Anne Aronson defines as "downward mobility" (39–40). Some of these parents have unrealistic expectations that their children will return to them unchanged by education, hence the fear my students often communicate to me of becoming alienated from their families. In the case of the Preston County women, however, most moved upward rather than downward, from earning no salary or from working at low-paying jobs to working in jobs with higher wages.

For many of these women, college graduation was the culmination of their families' great sacrifice and pride, the first cog in the spiral of influence. The true spirit of whistlin' and crowin' women especially came to fruition in Sarah's graduation, the result of Naomi's passing along her wisdom and desire for self-improvement.

College Literacy

Sarah enrolled in college after her son, born the last year she was in high school, enrolled in first grade. Her college literacy story is quite different from the stories of Lucy and Jean.

> Listening to my mother, I had to come to college. I waited seven years after high school until my son, Luke, was in first grade so that I could be with him in his early years. When he went to school, I knew where he was every day from 8 o'clock till 4 o'clock in the evening, so I enrolled at Preston College.
>
> I had no regrets about waiting to come to college because when I went back, I knew what I wanted. I knew where I was going. If I had been fresh out of high school, I wouldn't have done nearly as well because I wasn't focused and didn't know what I wanted. I have known for a long time that I wanted to work with abused and neglected children, so I majored in psychology and human services. I've always been a people person, and the summer before I started school, that major was just the area I wanted with all these reports of child abuse, child neglect, and so forth. And that's what drew me in that direction, besides the fact that I like working with kids.
>
> When I enrolled in English 111, I wasn't sure of my writing at the beginning. However, I did well, passed the proficiency easily, and ended up with an A for the class. I also did well in English 112 with another instructor. My response to the 1988 CBS *48 Hours* segment about a nearby Appalachian community, entitled "Looks Can Be Deceiving," was published in the student publication *Voices from*

the Hill. I am continually bothered by the media picturing us in one particular way, so I responded in the essay to the common stereotypes of the area: tightly knit families, shacks for housing, and early marriage.

The two religion classes I took at the college confirmed for me what Mother had always taught me about the Bible, that it has all kinds of stories—love, murder, intrigue, and so on.

I remember nothing negative about college except for horrible test anxiety. More specifically, I regret one math course in which I did not do as well as I had expected. From freshman to senior year, I felt more confident and had higher self-esteem. The more I progressed in school, the more confident I became that I could do it. Good grades meant more to me in college than in high school. I was bound and determined that I was going to graduate with honors, and I did. I performed well in all my classes and was a tenth of a point from graduating summa cum laude, so I graduated cum laude. I was able to complete my degree in four years because I went straight through two summers. My mother tells me that I am more independent, happier, and more willing to keep learning since college. Basically, I liked going back to school and learning new things.

When I would come home from college classes, my son, Luke, would call to me from the other room while I was fixing supper, "Mom, here's your song. Come and watch!" every time he saw the video of Reba McIntire's song "Is There Life Out There?" The video depicts a woman—who is married in her twenties with two children—going back to school and wondering if she has a life beyond her family and her home. So, in addition to my mother, Luke became my cheerleader, loving to go to the college for visits. I always put his schoolwork before my own, and after he had done his homework, had his bath, brushed his teeth, and gone to bed, it was my time. And sometimes my time was *all night.*

Though I had encouragement from Naomi and Luke, I did not have it from my second husband, Bill. He was a traditional man who wanted me to be more passive. He felt that he should be the breadwinner and felt that my being in college was a threat to his manhood in providing for his family. And after I started college, I didn't have as much time for him. So he sort of got pushed to the side a little bit. At one point, he asked me to choose between him and school. I told him not to make me decide because he'd lose. From that time on he did not pressure me again, but he was not wholly supportive.

Bill stayed with me during my college years, but we divorced in March 1998. During divorce proceedings, he told me that I had changed when I went to college. But I feel that he changed because he was always an insecure person, and during our marriage, I always had to Band-Aid his insecurities. When we were talking, he would say, "What does that mean? You're using words I don't understand. You're talking mumbo-jumbo. I don't know what you're talking about." If I had not gone to college, I would be sitting at home taking all the crap that Bill dished out. I wouldn't be able to support my son and myself. With college, I could say, "I'm a person too. I don't have to take this nonsense from my husband." Primarily, I feel that college contributed to my sense of independence and financial security, which in turn threatened my husband and had a direct effect on the divorce.

Unlike Jean and Lucy, Sarah had been a good student in high school, winning several awards at her graduation. She would probably have done just as well coming directly out of high school to college as her mother had hoped she would, though she says that she would not have had the focus she had seven years later. When I talked with faculty members about whom I was interviewing for my research, two of them said, "Oh, I had Sarah, and she was a model student."

What interested me in this interview was the enthusiasm Sarah's son shared with her and Naomi for her being in college, so much so that they had "their song." Like all the other informants, Sarah put her son's concerns before her own. Sarah's husband, Bill, was obviously threatened by her being in school, but he stayed with her during that time and for a short while afterward until he had an affair, which Sarah said was to prove his manhood and which "proved himself out of a relationship" (May 5, 1999).

Though I submitted several of Sarah's essays to *Voices from the Hill* during her time in my class, she did not have any accepted by the editor until she enrolled in English 112. As she described above, her essay (excerpted below) challenged the media stereotypes of this area as depicted in a CBS *48 Hours* episode.

> Finally, the program showed a young couple getting married. Before the ceremony took place, the interviewer talked with the bride and groom. The couple talked about how excited they were about getting married and later having babies. This portrayal implied that all the young people of Eastern Kentucky are hillbillies who just want to hurry and get married at an early age and have babies. Sure,

there are many young people who do get married and start a family immediately, but that happens everywhere. This does not mean that all Eastern Kentuckians marry by the time they are eighteen years old. For, example, I did not marry Bill until I was twenty years old. My friend Tara was twenty-eight years old before she married her husband Jason, and she did not have her first child until she was thirty. My Aunt Drew is forty years old and is still a single lady today. She says she hasn't found the right man yet.

Sarah handled her objections to the upsetting media portrayal of our region with graphic examples and even humor that make the essay strong. Knowing her emphasis on correctness, I can guess that this paper was almost letter perfect (see appendix G for full text).

Sarah performed well all four years and graduated with a 3.68 GPA. Reminding me of my own mother's pride in my studying for my doctorate, Sarah summarized her feelings at graduation, which paralleled her mother's:

I guess the one thing that made it [going to college] all seem worth it to me was on graduation day when my mom got to stand there and watch the dream come true. And just as soon as they started playing the music, my mom started crying. So that is what I worked hard for. Her dream and my dream. (Sarah, January 25, 1999)

I was sitting there [at Sarah's graduation], and I was saying, "That's my baby." And I'd say, "Is that really my baby doing that?" to myself. And I was so proud, I could hardly speak. She's the only one in our family that had ever graduated college. And she was the one with the least opportunity. The rest of her family had a mother, a father; they were working people. But their parents weren't as interested in them as I was in mine. And she was the least likely one to have graduated. But she was the only one that did. (Naomi, April 30, 1999)

Post-college Literacy: Workplace

In early April 1999, I observed Sarah's workplace literacy by returning to her office on the day she set aside for filling out her extensive paperwork. From this and her final interview, I gathered the
following information, which Sarah shares in narrative form. Having interviewed her in January, I knew that her office and the physical notes she took would be immaculate and up-to-date. For three
hours, Sarah discussed and shared blank forms with me as she conveyed the importance of precise records related to the care of her
clients, children who have been severely abused. She shares that
literacy below:

> Graduating cum laude from Preston College in May 1993,
> I treated myself to a summer of relaxation before looking for
> a job. My good grades and teacher recommendations netted
> me a job that October with the local administrative unit of
> the statewide mental health organization. In terms of prepa-
> ration for my job, I believe that the college gave me a firm
> foundation. I worked there with adults who had MRDD
> (mental retardation developmental disability) and SPD,
> which is severe psychiatric disorder. I trained these adults,
> but I also did vocational assessments, which was like writ-
> ing a comprehensive story, because you've got to know the
> clients' skills, limitations, and strengths. I wrote all of this
> information by hand on an assessment form. I worked at
> the mental health agency for four years.
>
> The reason I majored in psychology/human services was
> to serve children who couldn't fight for themselves, espe-
> cially severely abused foster care children, so I was happy
> to hear about the opening in fall 1997 for a foster care
> worker at Cobblestone Counseling Center, a center affiliated

with the state Baptist program for children. I joined two other caseworkers in October 1997. At the mental health group, I worked with adults. Here I work with children, so this is where I wanted to be. Being a single mom, I have to stay where the money is better, so that keeps me here.

The State Department of Community Based Services contracts with Cobblestone for care and placement of children removed from their homes; they are difficult to place in foster homes because of their severe emotional or physical problems. Kentucky Baptist Homes for Children has therapeutic homes throughout the state with experienced foster parents who have already been trained to deal with kids that have difficulties.

We get the tough cases. Each child in foster care has a rating; two of the six in my caseload are worst-case scenario or level five. One was six years old; one was almost eighteen. Most of the children in my care have been abused or molested, and all are placed in counseling as soon as they are placed in foster care. It's a shame what parents do to their children; they need to start very early with them if they're going to turn out to be any type of decent human being. The reason they become so hard-core is because of the coping skills they've acquired to deal with their unbearable experiences.

Paperwork. My supervisor says, "If you didn't record it, it didn't happen!" So I am a careful person about detail and have devised several ways to keep accurate notes. Using my three calendar day-planners, notebooks, and phone, fax, and data from home visits, I gather information and transfer it to various forms. I choose one day of each month near the beginning of the month to complete these forms on the agency laptop. For my records, I keep a floppy disk and a hard copy that goes into each child's notebook.

Foster Parent Forms. Because these children need good solid homes to be placed in, one crucial part of my job is to identify strong and reliable foster parents. So one of the forms I might fill out is a Preliminary Information Sheet on possible foster parents that asks them about their age, highest grade completed, marital status and years married, occupation, and church affiliation. The remaining information requested pertains to personality, conflict resolution patterns, quality of their marriage, disciplinary techniques, and other factors that point to adequate care of foster children.

Because Cobblestone is a Baptist-affiliated institution, the agency is interested in the foster parents' religion, so we ask about denomination, church attendance, and involvement. The couple or parent does not have to be Baptist, but the agency does expect some sort of religious affiliation since their ministry is Christian. Though most foster children go to services every Sunday with their families, we don't force religion on these kids, and none has been resistant so far to attending church with their foster families.

After we conduct and write up the home study on the foster families, we talk with the foster care director, the family services director, and the regional administrator who all sign approval of the form. Once the agency identifies the family (single parents are acceptable), the agency provides forty-two hours of special training, which includes behavioral techniques of discipline, ways to physically restrain children should they become uncontrollable, and other skills. At the end of training, there is a "skill-out" where the parents demonstrate their newly learned skills. Once approved, the foster parents renew their training yearly.

Knowing how to read and write is essential for foster parents who must keep daily written logs which describe their daily events, for example, if the children played sports or helped with certain tasks around the house. It's documentation to show what they and the children have done daily, together and separately. When I visit the families weekly, I look at these reports.

Sarah's job is connected to taking children out of abusive homes and placing them in a safe and caring environment. That necessitates the identification of superior candidates for foster parents who must be able to read and write, handle conflicts and discipline, and house the children adequately. Because this agency's mission is to provide "Christ-centered ministry to provide care and hope for hurting children and families through the financial support of the commonwealth's southern Baptist churches" (Smithwick), the foster parents' faith is important, though that in itself would not qualify them. It may be that the discipline of going to church provides these drifting children with a direction. Sarah's literacy teamed up with foster parents' literacy assist the agency in providing good care for these troubled children.

Foster Children's Forms. For each child in my care, I have to fill out the Treatment Review Form. On it, I record family contact, emotions and behaviors, relationships and social skills, education, recreation, spirituality, and physical health. When I make a home visit to the foster parents, I get the information to place on that form by filling out the

Home Visit Checklist, which details the foster home I visited, the date of the visit, and who was present. If I go by the
house and no one is at home, I write "ATTEMPT" on the form,
and under assessment: "No one was home at this time."

Every three months, I fill out a Comprehensive Individual Treatment Plan for each of the children in my care.
This form most particularly applies to the child's psychological and environmental problems, emotional and developmental concerns, family concerns, and educational or
employment issues.

Because these children come from abusive backgrounds,
they can, during the time they are in foster care, commit
infractions. If any of them is involved in any of thirty-four
possible incidents, such as AWOL with whereabouts unknown, drug trafficking, possession of a deadly weapon,
sexually perpetrating or assaulting others, or official report
of sexual, mental, emotional, or physical neglect, I will fill
out a Client Incident Report. On that form, I might recommend any of twenty-four possible actions to resolve the incident, including referral for medical treatment, seclusion,
transfer to another unit, termination, hospitalization for
psychiatric or medical evaluation, or referral to law enforce-
ment. I have filled one of these out on several clients, like
the girl who took off without permission and nobody knew
where she was. She and her friend had stolen and damaged
a car and ended up in Ohio and then Georgia. We got them
for habitual runaway, and they had to go to court. Because
this girl had done it more than once within a certain period of time, she spent some time in detention.

When the foster children are originally removed from their biological parents' homes and placed in foster care, one of our goals is to rehabilitate the parent(s) so that the children might return home. As the social worker, I observe if those parents have conformed to treatment goals with Community Based Services within a twelve-month period, since they are evaluated twice during the year. In one case we have three kids whose mom has failed to meet any of her treatment goals. She has made no effort to make contact with her kids in this time period, so I can initiate the TPR (Termination of Parental Rights) as long as the children's counselor and therapist recommend it.

When a child leaves foster care either because his or her biological parents fulfilled state requirements for acceptable changes or when he or she turned eighteen and is therefore considered an adult, I fill out a Service Termination Form A. These children can go back home, do what they want to do, or decide to do extended commitment to the care, which allows them to get some type of vocational training or college. What truly saddens me is that many of these children have no home to return to.

It is obvious to me that the agency in general and Sarah in particular care for each child in their charge, considering all aspects of the child's personality and behavior as well as psychological and physical health. Her job requires close cooperation with foster parents and other agencies who deliver service to the children. Sarah has weekly staff meetings with her co-workers and also meets with outside groups like the court system and the biological parents from whom the child was taken. During my observation, she shared a particularly distressing story of a client who came into her care pregnant.

When the client had her baby, the baby became a client, and Sarah had to have the baby removed from the mother's care because of the mother's drug usage. The mother was given six months to show progress before the baby would be returned to her. We can see why Sarah retreats to the comfort of her house, her son, and mother when she returns home from work so as to recover from the emotional toll of seeing these children suffer.

Writing. Record-keeping is a crucial part of serving these children in the best way possible, so I am thorough about my notes. I keep a three-inch-thick notebook for each foster child. At the front of the notebook, I have a copy of the Client's Review Survey, which includes a list of all possible forms in the notebook; I check the ones included for that child. I am obsessive about using my day-planner to keep notes in when I am out in the field, waiting until my return to the office before I fill out the agency forms. In addition, I record the times of home visits, medical information about clients, and the results of phone calls. A typical page from my day-planner might look like this:

> completed A's discharge
> T___ approved
> PMH [hospital] drug screen
> fax
> h.v. [home visit]
> paperwork due
> client SSI [social security insurance]
> appt [appointment] at office
> have directions faxed to office

In the notebook I carry, I have a list of common client misbehaviors, treatment goals, objectives, target dates, interventions, staff responsibility, and outcomes. In addition,

I carry a copy of a sample of a discharge summary, a copy of an annual foster home evaluation, the child/youth supplement, the list of current treatment plans, and sample goals and objectives for foster parents. Two other foster care workers sign off on the treatment plans.

In addition to typing my staff notes, I keep a computer disk with each category of forms. In addition to this notebook, I keep a plastic accordion folder filled with all kinds of information, primarily notes on all the clients whom the agency serves. This information helps me respond to client needs when I am on call on every third weekend, when I carry an on-call pager.

My carefully written records assist me during monthly meetings with the treatment review team, which is made up of three foster care workers, the supervisor, and the treatment support worker, who works half-time to cover situations that we full-time staff cannot get to. I also share information in my monthly meeting with the child's counselor. Then, every three months, I meet with the child's social worker from the Department of Social Services. When the foster children in my care become involved in an altercation or when parental rights need to be terminated, I work closely with the court systems in surrounding counties.

Because filling out so many forms and reports without being repetitious can be difficult, I work hard to be creative and accurate with my staff notes with the result that my writing abilities have in fact been evaluated as one of my strengths. I truly become impatient with all the poorly written communications from staff and the higher-ups. I am usually asked to compose memos or letters that need to go out from the agency to foster parents or outside agencies. Others in the agency seek me out when they are having writing problems. Anytime they want a certain type of memo or letter written up, I end up having to write it because my wording and writing skills are better than some around here. Reading departmental memos, I cannot stand certain errors, like fragments and comma splices. It DRIVES ME UP THE WALL, especially if the person writing it has a college degree.

Sarah's on-the-job writing was extensive: she filled out weekly, monthly, quarterly, and annual reports (see table 5 for a list of forms). In addition, she read charts of other foster children posted by her co-workers and evaluation reports from court and psychological services. To keep herself organized, she read and wrote in her daily planner. Because she was known for her writing skills (and had been commended for them by her supervisor), she was often asked to write outgoing letters to agencies, foster parents, and other officials. The same emphasis on correctness that I saw in English composition carried over to Sarah's workplace literacy. Once she became reconnected with correct grammar and essay construction, Sarah

Table 5. Sarah's Foster Care Forms

Name of Form	When Completed
Preliminary Information Sheet (on foster parents)	as needed
Treatment Review Form (for child)	monthly
Home Visit Checklist (family)	weekly or per visit
Client Incident Report (child)	as needed
Comprehensive Individual Treatment Plan	every three months
Service Termination Form A	as child leaves foster care
Termination of Parental Rights	as needed
Client's Review Survey	list of all possible forms in notebook

was sometimes more correct than she was creative. Students like her are a challenge for a writing teacher who needs to emphasize the flexibility of language as well as the rules of the written code. Her impatience with others for whom writing and correct grammar are not important reminded me of Peter Trudgill's study of Norwich working-class families, especially the women who paid more attention to detail in the hopes that it would help them raise their status. This impatience reflects her comfort with the written code, which not all of her co-workers share.

Reading. Besides the writing I do, I have to keep up with my reading. To work with the client and fill in the Comprehensive Individual Treatment Plan, I have to be able to read the *Diagnostic and Statistical Manual,* a thick tome that classifies and describes all mental disorders. To be a good team member for treatment reviews, I have to read other foster care workers' reports since all of us work together in this small office and need information about clients who might call during our on-call time. I read some of the psychological evaluations that come in. We also have a lot more reading when we are writing up reports.

One way for me to improve myself is to begin graduate work. I am working toward a master's in social work, which the University of Kentucky is offering at a satellite location nearby. Though I am not opposed to moving away from the area to get a better job, I want to wait until Luke is out of school so that he has some permanence until he graduates from high school.

Post-college Literacy: Home

Since visiting Sarah's home was not part of the original methodology (and I visited Lucy's home only because she did not work outside the home), I asked in our final interview what I would see in the way of literacy if I came to her home. I was hoping to get as complete a picture as possible of home-based literacy.

Since college, my reading and writing habits have not changed too much, since I do as much now as I did in college. Before college, I mostly read Harlequin and historical romances and magazines; now I have no time for stuff like that. At home, even my casual reading is related to the children and foster parents I work with. On my bookshelves at home are these titles: *Kids Have Feelings Too, Depression, The Angry Teenager,* and several math, reading, and curriculum books that I have loaned to foster parents whose children were having trouble in those areas.

There are some math books and a few history books. I am busy, but if I have time to read, I will pick up something like self-help and self-exploration books like *Co-dependent No More* or *Self-Taught,* which also help me with my clients. If I read anything else, I like stories based on real-life events, like a book based on a murder in a nearby Kentucky town, and *The FBI Killer,* written about the FBI agent who killed his informant in Preston County. I keep up with local news by reading the triweekly newspaper and my mail. For recreation, I love to fish because it takes me to a place where I don't have to think, just rest, so I subscribe to some fishing magazines.

In terms of community literacy, I don't do anything in the community. It's intense working with severely abused children, and I need a total break from being with anyone more than Mother and family. I am on call every third weekend.

If Luke has a school function, I will probably attend, and I joined the PTA when he was in elementary school. Outside of these connections to the community, I am not active.

Since at work I always use a computer, I tend to play on it at home, and Luke has taught me everything I need to know. Because I cannot get away from work to do my chores, I use the computer at home to communicate in writing with my landlord, attorney, and other businesses. I'll sit down and do a letter form on the computer and do my own letterhead and design my own thing because usually by the time I get home, offices are closed, and so I just write them letters. With my many daily planners, I am constantly writing, keeping a calendar of events.

Sarah's home literacy reflected her work-related interests as well as her recreation. She described to me how she designed a letterhead and sent business letters out to attorneys (see figure 4), landlords, and others she could not call during the day. She liked spending time with her son, who operated as her teacher in home-related activities on the computer. Her computer use was similar to the other seven participants' use. Owning a personal computer was also an indicator of how well some of them were doing financially in comparison to the homes they grew up in. Polly's family played strategy games on the computer and used it for e-mail. Mary wrote poetry and personal thoughts out in a journal of sorts on the computer when something bothered her; "if you don't want to talk to somebody about it, it helps to write about it" (February 2, 1999). Judith used the computer for her lesson plans and other school activities.

Sarah's Summary

I believe that the qualities of an educated person are life experience, openness to change, and the willingness to

December 17, 1998

RE:
          Circuit Court, Action No.

Dear Mr.

        Enclosed you will find an agreement that I will settle for out of
court regarding my recent divorce. Therefore, I need for you to
present these things to Bill 's attorney,   so that we
can finally get this whole thing over and done with.

        If you have any questions or concerns, feel free to contact me at
home or at work. My work number is   I appreciate
you for all your assistance in the past and in the future.

Sincerely,

                                              (both parties teenage son)
                        1.   I want full custody of
                        2.   Bill will have standard visitation rights.
                        3.   - Bill will continue to pay $300.00 monthly child support until
Enclosure   . graduates from high school. Currently, Luke is 15 years
                                of age (date of birth is January 17th) and a Sophomore at
                                Central High School. Payments will cease to exist after the month of
                                high school graduation because Luke will turn 18 years of age six
                                months before his expected high school graduation. As we all know,
                                the senior year is the most expense year of school. Therefore, Bill
                                will only have 2 ½ years of financial obligations.
                        4.   Bill will continue to provide medical insurance for . Luke and
                                will be responsible for any expense that is not covered by the medical
                                coverage if the expense pertains to any medical treatment that is out of
                                the ordinary as described by the medical insurance. In addition,
                                Bill will sign the insurance checks over to me that is reimbursed by
                                the insurance company regarding Luke because this money will be
                                paid in advanced by the child support.
                        5.   I will continue to provide dental insurance on Luke as long as it is
                                available to me through the company where I work. I will be
                                responsible for any dental bills that are not covered by this insurance.
                        6.   Both parties will assist as much as possible with any college or
                                vocational expenses that are reasonable.

Fig. 4. Sarah's letter to her attorney

Previous Savings Account:
1. There will be no division of money due to the depletion of this
    account for various reasons as presented to the court previously.

Marital Possessions:
1. I will be granted full ownership of the 1990 Chevy Cavalier, which
    has been paid for since April, 1994. I will accept full responsibility of
    any expense regarding said car.

2. Bill will continue to have full ownership of his 1993 Chevy S-10
    pickup truck and will continue to assume full responsibility of any
    expenses for said truck.

3. Bill can pay me half of the value of the 1979 Bass boat or the boat
    can be sold and the profit divided among both parties.

4. I will have full ownership of the outdoor building. Bill has already
    taken ALL his personal belongings out of the building such as his
    hunting and fishing equipment, tools, etc.

5. I will continue to have full ownership of ALL home upkeep tools such
    as lawnmower, weedeater, etc.

6. I will continue to have full ownership of ALL household furnishings.

7. I will continue to have full possession of the parties 1997 mobile
    home that is currently located at .   . Ky. Bill will continue to
    pay $250.00 as he has for the past year to assist in providing our son a
    home until he graduates from high school. I will be allowed to move
    the location of the said home at my expense if I choose to do so
    in the future. The mortgage payment at this time is approximately
    $355.00 a month. I will continue to pay the lot rent of $125.00, which
    will be about equal money in providing our son a home. However, if I
    should remarry, the home will be my full responsibility or if I choose
    not to keep the home, it will be sold and any profit will be equally
    split between Bill and myself. In addition, I will continue as I have
    for the past year to be responsible for the mobile home's insurance
    coverage. Both parties will equally pay any property taxes until our
    son graduates from high school. Finally, both parties' names will
    remain on the title and on the mortgage payment until our son
    graduates from high school. At that time, Bill will remove his
    name from the title and he will no longer be responsible for the
    mortgage if the home is not sold.

experience new things. I can tell you that without college, I would probably still be married to my husband who was always throwing up to me, "You're too independent." He would have loved for me to stay dependent on him. But I wasn't raised that way. And I guess that gives me a lot of self-satisfaction. But since he's been gone, my son and I have a new car, we still have our home, and we pay our own insurance. We've not been late with any bills. I am bound and determined I will be successful. And I am moving closer to my goal. With my master's in social work, I will be more employable, successful, and independent, just like Mom hoped I would be.

Lessons

Sarah taught me about the need to balance my classroom teaching to include students like Sarah who do so well that teachers might often neglect them for the students who do poorly. The challenge for teaching these kinds of students is to be able to illustrate the flexibility of the written code as it grows and changes just like any living thing. Often such students worry so much about correctness that they forget to listen to their own voices and creativity. Sarah's intensity and determination to succeed held her in good stead academically, and she was building on the foundation with good work experience and continuing education opportunities. She had shown Naomi that she could live independently, just as Naomi had done in raising Sarah by herself, and in the winter of 1999, Sarah was trying to pass that legacy along to her son, illustrating the intergenerational effects of literacy.

I spoke with Sarah recently, and she informed me that her son had gone away to college but could not stand being away from home, so he was back home. She has married again, to a man who seems to respect her independence. She is working in an advisory capacity with Preston College to create a bachelor's in social work, a major that she believed would make PC graduates more employable. From the time of the original interview, she has held two other jobs, one as director of an agency similar to Cobblestone, and now as case manager in an area mental health agency. She continues to work toward getting her MSW, knowing that advanced learning is something she will do well in. At the end of our interview, Sarah said, "I don't know if it's to prove to the world or prove to myself that I'm going to make it" (May 5, 1999). There is no doubt that Sarah will go far and that Naomi will continue to be proud of her daughter. (See table 6 for Sarah's post-college literacy practices.)

Table 6. Post-college Literacy Practices: Sarah

Work	*Reading: Diagnostic and Statistical Manual,* log that foster care family keeps, psychological evaluations from counselor, reports on clients of co-workers, departmental memos, daily planners
	Writing: three daily planners (well organized); weekly, monthly, quarterly, and annual reports; notebook; completed home study of foster parents; forms; imaginative staff notes
	Job Advancement: Courses toward a master's degree in social work
	Technology: Fax, phone, laptop at work, floppy disks for records
Home	*Reading:* encyclopedias, true life crime books, old texts, fishing magazines, triweekly paper, counseling and self-help books
	Writing: daily planners
	Technology: uses computer to design letterhead and compose letters to businesses, lawyer, landlord.

Conclusion

I had the fear, honey. I was scared to death. Being in there with
kids that were younger than my own kids. Sometimes I'd say,
"What am I doing here?"

—Judith (February 5, 1999)

Coming to Good Ends

Fear silences. Fear paralyzes. I look at my fears in the past: fear of
moving to Kentucky from Maryland, fear of earning my master's in
English at the age of forty-two, fear of beginning my doctoral program at the age of fifty. Fear of failure outweighed the fear of success, but fear silenced me. Through faith, I learned to step out of
fear, to stir the silence, and ultimately to achieve my goals. But if I
had failed in any of those endeavors, I had the strong arms of my
spouse to comfort me. If I had failed, I had extended family supporting me. If I had failed, I had chances for other opportunities and
options because of my class and my education. If I had failed, I could
still hold my head high because my spouse and I are recognized in
our community. If I had failed, I would not risk being unable to put
food on my family's table.

So when I heard Judith, one of the eight Preston County women,
tell me about fear and add her observation to the narratives of Lucy,
Jean, Sarah, Polly, Mary, Faith, and Hope, I began to understand the
fears that silenced them when they entered Preston College for the
first time. Climbing the literal and figurative ninety-nine steps to the
college, surrounded by traditional students fresh out of high school,
they were making sacrifices far riskier than my own. As they stepped
into academic discourse, their failure had deeper consequences: failing would mean facing family and relatives who had not supported
their enrollment to start out with, failing would mean continuing
to work minimum wage jobs, and failing would mean the inability

to support their families. Like me, the eight women confronted their fears, faced the academic challenges, surmounted internal and external obstacles, and achieved what they wanted.

They, like me, learned that they were more intelligent than they thought and that they had something to offer the world beyond the divided roles of spouses, mothers, and workers. They strived to achieve their goals because the alternatives were just not viable. Their silence turned to noise as they heard their voices, and those voices blend with women across the nation, including Dominican women in New York City (Sterling-Deer), Russian Old Believer women in Alaska (Graber), and Lakota Indian women (Gutwein), to broadcast the strength of marginalized women. They prove that "learning leads to some type of fundamental change in the learners' sense of themselves, their worldviews, their understanding of their pasts, and their orientation to the future" (Brooks 140). They illustrate the coming to voice through education that built on their innate literacy and survival skills in a largely patriarchal society to show that women can overcome fears to come to good ends. Ultimately, the women of eastern Kentucky's stories upset our notions of feminism and class and teach us how we can teach better.

Although I knew these women were special when they were in my classroom, until these interviews I had never imagined the extent of their sacrifices in attending college. I became reacquainted with their native intelligence, cultural savvy, and self-sufficiency that sustained them and assisted them in their success. These women were not "helpless victims . . . or possessors of idealized virtue" (Rowbotham 51), and they were not entirely voiceless within the context of their families, but they wanted "to speak for themselves and have their voices listened to; they want to become independent and to control their own lives" (Clarenbuch qtd. in Rotkis and McDaniel 318). These interviews woke me up to my classism, and so as a "professor-learner" (Hamilton 139), I conclude this book with the lessons I learned by relating pedagogy to the concept of voice as language, identity, and power and by suggesting some implications for collegewide responses to nontraditional students.

Lessons Learned

Voice as Language

I have learned from these women to respect the dialect and vernacular of my students, and I ask my students to share with me their ways of knowing. Spoken language is no indicator of intelligence, and applying the rules of the written code to spoken language is another language prejudice (Milroy and Milroy). Scholars have shown that dialect interference in writing is minimal (Hartwell), and yet academics still see language deficit and place blame on students for their writing problems, which continues to keep them from excelling in the academy. Even if students improve linguistically, some teachers rarely change attitudes about such students, and those students begin to internalize self-hate, try to speak the dominant discourse, and downgrade themselves in the process. In the meantime, they limit their school achievement, become more powerless, take on low expectations, and learn to be helpless (Edwards and Giles). Jennifer Horsman's study of literacy supports this point:

> The student's own language comes to seem incorrect which can easily lead to students seeing themselves as inferior . . . and goes a long way toward explaining how school has been a place of silencing and becoming "stupid" for working-class children from many communities. (13)

Linguists hope to correct this problem by making teachers more aware of how language discrimination maintains an unequal balance and distribution of power.

Creating awareness of ways of speaking and making choices depending on purposes of language use are among the goals I have in my Appalachian dialect unit in the first-year composition class. I work to make students aware of the dignity of Appalachian English as they bring vocabulary and aphorisms to class to share and discuss. While the students and I examine how outsiders stereotype Appalachia based on the spoken language, I have them list stereotypes of other regions, like the northeast, and point to positive and negative uses of stereotypes. They learn to recognize the different requirements and purposes of spoken and written language. They soon recognize that speakers do not all speak one way; even as nonstandard speakers, students shift between Standard and nonstandard English. Any activities like this in the classroom affirm students' ways of speaking and help to bridge the gap between spoken and written language. When Preston College added a football team made up largely of African American males from South Carolina and Georgia, a tennis team made up of Latin Americans, and a baseball team made up of Puerto Ricans, I changed the name of the unit from "Appalachian dialect" to the broader "language awareness." Respect for language can lead to more self-confidence for nonstandard and second language speakers of English.

Voice as Identity

Students' ways of speaking reveal one part of their identities and relate closely to social class identity. Just as teachers have attitudes toward nonstandard speakers of English, so they discriminate on the basis of class, though often unintentionally. Although not all working-class students have a difficult time in the writing classroom (Ashley), some do because they have been passed over in the public school that is geared to preparing middle- and upper-income students to succeed in college. Many working-class women work hard to move their families forward by seeking education for their children. Some say that acquiring academic identity creates a sense of erasure. Though the Preston County women experienced some resistance from family, they resolved the fissures and returned to their communities, confirming that "academic success [does not] depend upon breaking our students' ties with their communities or that the denial of a working-class background is the price to pay for academic success and upward mobility" (Pari 140–41). Eileen Ferretti echoes this feeling about working-class women in her class who found "a voice of their own" in higher learning: "I do not believe that the construction of a student identity . . . necessitates the erasure of other existing identities" (84). Specifically, this research has illustrated for me that teacher attitudes like my own, which assumed that all working-class students aspire to middle-class values and want to move out of their surroundings, are elitist (Pari).

One of the most effective means for helping nontraditional women to discover multiple identities is personal writing. In this study, the biggest part of the Preston County women's identity rested in their ability to write, to redefine their multiple selves and record stories, to learn how to organize a piece to be readable by an audience, and to express their personal feelings and thoughts. The women wrote about what they knew and were

> more rooted in the interpersonal relationships and caretaking activities [that] they participate in at home and limited by the subordinate roles they play in the workplace . . . inscrib[ing] their live experiences as wives, mothers, and working women. (Ferretti 84)

Like the women Deborah Piper taught, the Preston County women built on those life experiences and revealed "incredible talents and strengths . . . as they wrote of finding ways to advocate for themselves and their communities. . . . All became empowered by their own stories" (289–90). Writing operated as a vehicle for opening up voices that are often "suppressed, silenced, marginalized, written out of what counts for authoritative knowledge" (Flynn 551).

Though all women are not the same, most of the women responded to developmental and interpersonal writing, which is not as privileged in the academy as disembodied, academic discourse. I think it crucial that compositionists work to integrate "classroom practices which promote an understanding of self as writer" (Brooke, *Writing* 5) so that any writing that follows has integrity. Being able to share stories creates this self-definition, something most of these women have never had a chance to do. In doing so, they are like the adult education students in Wendy Luttrell's study whose experience "afforded . . . some the opportunity to revisit and reinterpret past feelings of powerlessness and inadequacy . . . [and establish] a credible, worthy self and public identity" (20, 126). Compositionists do not want to deny students access to learning about academic writing, which they need in other classes, but writing expressively is a foundation on which to build for many working-class students.

The value of writing is that it "helps them [the women] understand and interact with their community" (Brooke, *Writing* 6). Just as I created awareness of dialect, so I can introduce the subject of working-class "languages, cultures and knowledge at the center of the writing classroom [which] can enrich and improve the learning experiences of . . . marginalized groups" (Pari 140). That sense of self can be used to bridge the gap from personal to academic writing and eventually from there to workplace literacy, but beginning with the personal is a good first step, especially for nontraditional women.

Voice as Power

Coming to a new identity as literate residents of eastern Kentucky, the Preston County women achieved power by building on past literacies and by "accumulating literacy," which Deborah Brandt defines as "[horizontal] layers of earlier forms of literacy [that] exist simultaneously within the society and within the experiences of individuals" or as vertical layers of reading and writing documents in the workplace and at home ("Accumulating" 652). This accumulation "provides an increasingly intricate set of incentives, sources, and barriers for learning to read and write, the negotiation of which becomes a large part of the effort of becoming (and staying) literate" (665). In my interviews, I found that these mountain women conveyed a rich background from their early literacy. Since the women came to college with the ability to read and write on a certain level, they built on it with academic and other literacies.

These layers of literacy began at home where they saw literacy modeled by their parents, especially biblical literacy. In addition, Hope reported seeing her mother teach her dad to read; Faith saw her father reading Louis L'Amour westerns and *National Geographic;* Sarah's mother traveled to the public library monthly to bring home boxes of books, especially biblical commentaries; and all participants were actively involved with extended family in reading the Bible. Lucy remembered her mother's poetry, and Judith's mother wrote letters to relatives away from Preston County. In elementary school, these women made regular trips to the library and wrote book reports; in high school they rarely wrote.

The Preston County women built on their practical literacy skills by choosing practical majors. Lucy reported that she began as a social work major until she discovered in her first basic art class that she could use her hands to create paintings and sculptures. Jean became a nurse after taking care of her elderly grandmother. Sarah, always interested in righting the wrongs she observed in her community, chose to serve abused children by becoming a social worker. The other five women studied to be teachers and reported that the courses that stood out for them used practical activities to convey course content to the children they would teach. Writing occurred in the form of journals, poetry, and essays in language arts classes; essay exams and research papers in the social science and humanities courses; and in the required two-sequence composition course. Reading took place in all disciplines and gave two of the eight extreme difficulties throughout their four years.

The power of literacy rested in its uses for these women in the workplace. As city clerk, Polly learned the bookkeeping system of the woman who preceded her. She screened the mayor's calls, wrote messages, sent out bills and property taxes to residents, kept the books, and read ordinances and minutes of city council meetings. The women who were teachers—Judith, Hope, and Faith—wrote lesson plans, curriculum guidelines, and Individual Education Plans as well as materials to prepare for teaching. Mary, a data entry clerk for the environmental testing lab, used reading to look up information related to lab samples that came in and used writing to write up the report for the clients. At work, Sarah and Jean filled in forms related to clients and patients.

After finishing college, their uses for reading and writing at home varied. Socially, they interacted with their children by reading to them and helping them with their homework. Recreationally, they read novels, theme magazines (fishing, soap operas, digests), and material on the computer. Mary reported that she read more than she watched TV and liked John Grisham, Danielle Steel, John

Steinbeck, and many Appalachian authors. Lucy read stories from *Barney Magazine* and worked crossword puzzles with her children. Lucy, Jean, and Sarah used literacy extensively at home to supplement work-related activities: Lucy read about her daughter's disease; Jean read to supplement knowledge on illnesses of patients and to review for continuing education courses; Sarah read to learn more about how to deal with her clients.

It appears that writing continues to be important and vital in their lives. The Preston women used writing for communicating with family members and friends, keeping up with the news, understanding their workplace, gathering information, and improving their spiritual lives. In terms of literacy development since college, the whistlin' and crowin' women of Appalachia were doing well. Among the eight original participants, two write on their jobs (the teachers do more reading than writing except for lesson plans). Those going on for job advancement recognize that learning takes place in context; education majors cannot move on to the next rank in salary without more university courses. Acquiring advanced degrees takes literacy development one step further by expanding their knowledge in the field and in many cases equates to pay raises. Jean's work via correspondence courses toward a master's in critical care nursing and Sarah's work toward her master's in social work also had more to do with personal pride and achievement than pay. By improving literacy and self-confidence, the college supported women in their roles in the community, enhanced their skills in the area of mothering, and initiated the growing process in which learning is a lifelong process, all of which equated to power and voice. Like the women in southeastern Virginia, these women learned to

> interact with people different than themselves, [gain] new understandings of their lives and experiences, [make] new friends, [gain] increased confidence and willingness to speak . . . making a commitment to working for change in the community. (Bingman 219)

In processing the data I gathered about the Preston County women, I puzzled about how the results fit into feminist thought. Kimberley Donehower challenges me to see the paradox of strong women being made stronger by pursuing literacy at the college level and yet the persistence of the patriarchal society in which they have to live ("Re: thanks"). Others have pointed out that the women enter traditional work, which keeps them in low-paying positions. Many view the Preston County women as downtrodden and oppressed and see them as victims in a depressed economy.

While acknowledging that these women are twice silenced by gender and class, I have difficulty with others labeling them as downtrodden when they may not feel that way themselves; these "assumptions of subordination" can limit research and ignore context (Reinharz 119, 121). I interviewed these women to call attention to rural values, which are sometimes overlooked by "the best educated and most idealistic of first world women" who tend to look more at "the status problems of their own class" than to consider the struggles of rural women (Boulding 9–10). The Preston County women were concerned about the general economic conditions in the region for men and women and thus found it difficult to see the issues purely in feminist terms.

Several studies support my findings that education empowered women and improved their lives. Beth Daniell states that her Appalachian women were feminists in the narrow sense of "regarding women as fully human" and "embrac[ing] the conviction that men and women should share the power or that women should and can have choices in their own lives," but "they eschew aggressive public political stances or declarations of superiority over other people including but not limited to men" (*Communion* 147). In fact, most Appalachian men and women avoid strong stances and get their points across in other ways. The women in my study, as well, resisted the feminist label because of its radical connections and because they saw feminism as a middle- or upper-class movement. This resistance reflected what Ferretti discovered in her working-class women; they typically harbor some resentment toward highly educated professional women, and they cringe at the word "feminism." Although most of them came of age during the recent women's movement, they did not have access to the wider educational and professional options that their middle-class counterparts fought for. (78)

Daniell goes on to espouse the subtle power that these women yield, making a difference in their relationships and communities, for "politics at its most basic is what happens between human beings. . . . The personal . . . is political" (148).

Another study challenging the belief that education stratifies women, Gillian Pascall and Roger Cox's study of women returning to college, illustrates that women looked to education "to escape from the web in which many felt caught—looking for income and a career that could be combined with domestic responsibilities" (143). Ultimately, the way to counter the argument of education continuing to marginalize women is to look at how the women in these studies adapted education to their own needs and ends and at how education "played a key role in enabling new choices to be made about the balance between private and public life" (143).

Ultimately, coming to empowerment does not necessarily

spark collective change. The heightened awareness that individuals obtain from such [educational] practices can generate confidence and feelings of worth, but if transformation occurs, it may only be actualized on an individual basis. (Qualley 34–35)

D. J. Qualley urges us to begin dialogue so that women see what societal changes need to be made to make circumstances better for all women. For now, they fight their individual battles and advance women's causes in nonspecific ways.

The eight women in my study are feminist in the sense of having more opportunities and choices, which their college literacy gave them, and in their "family values [which] include a desire for growth, a courageous confronting of what stands in their way, and, above all, the imperative to create better conditions for their children" without destroying their communities (Kendrick). Perhaps their daughters will push beyond their mothers for more equity, but for now, the Preston County women are making a start.

Implications for Teachers

> Ethnographic knowing is a different sort of knowing; nevertheless, there is a shared theme of outsiders coming to know the insides of things.
>
> —Ralph Cintron, *Angels' Town*

As Researchers

Debate about how to label this teacher research exists. Cintron appears to give me permission to call the study ethnographic since I have lived in the field for so long and had developed trust that a researcher coming for a shorter period of time would not have been able to do. Shulamit Reinharz might label my research ethnographic because my methods "rely on the researcher's immersion in social setting, and aim for intersubjective understanding between researchers and the person(s) studied" (46), though in fact I did not immerse myself in the same sense as a true ethnographer might have. She goes on to say that "ethnography is an important feminist method if it makes women's lives visible, just as interviewing is an important feminist method if it makes women's voices audible" (48). Wendy Bishop might say that I have conducted a qualitative study using ethnographic techniques since I "cannot claim to study the culture from the culture's point of view" (36) because of my role as their former teacher and someone born outside the culture. I would settle the debate by stating that I have used "naturalistic observation," which "allows the inquirer to see the world as his [or her] subjects see it, to live in their time frames, to capture the phenomenon in and on its own terms, and to grasp the culture in its own natural, ongoing environment" (Guba and Lincoln 193). However it is labeled, the study offers a glimpse of literacy in action among a marginalized and underrepresented group, Appalachian women. Like all qualitative studies, the results are not meant to be generalized.

Experiencing these stories, I felt that I came to know the "insides" of the eight women's lives. More than anything, this research has taught me to be more observant of students of all ages in my own classroom and to take stock of my own "personal perceptions and deceptions, the ethnocentrism of [my] own mental baggage" (Luttrell 202). Especially as a teacher-researcher, I tried to "become more sensitive about how and in what ways [I] may be showing preferential treatment" (123) toward traditional middle-class Caucasian students and to become more aware of institutional practices and policies that validate some students at the expenses of others.

Teacher research like this can examine "the contextual worlds of their [our students'] day-to-day lives" (Luttrell 203) and offer teachers the chance for more student-centered changes in academic curriculum, policies, and procedures that affect nontraditional students. For I believe with David Barton and Mary Hamilton that

> the special value of research is the insights it can generate which go beyond the particular which it deals with, to extend out from the study and relate the local and the global. . . . Taken together such studies can offer a powerful challenge to dominant and simplifying discourses of literacy, and support the recognition of multiple literacies within educational and social policy. (264–65)

More than any other activity, these interviews with my former students enabled me to examine my prejudices and improve my teaching.

As Caregivers

What these stories demonstrate is that teachers can attend to the "caregiving side of teaching and learning" (Luttrell 124–25). This kind of teaching responds particularly to needs of nontraditional female students by valuing their mothering skills—the common sense and competence they have gained from raising children. They do not want to lose their identity as mothers, and they certainly do not need it devalued any more than it has been in the wider society and particularly in the public school, especially among working-class women. In fact, Luttrell cautions "against any program which would deny . . . women's wishes for intellectual mastery independent of the needs of children for whom they are primarily responsible" (126).

Recognizing that women returning to the classroom do not come empty-handed or -minded, teachers might identify gifts and talents of individual students before literacy instruction begins. Teachers might also recognize that women experience learning as "deeply personal and highly significant . . . as a source of personal growth" (Hayes and Flannery 76). Class and individual discussion and literacy narratives are excellent tools to begin that process.

Teachers need to be aware of academic literacy's limitations within the total picture of the literacies students have accumulated throughout their lives. Knowing that most women gain knowledge in diverse ways but particularly by seeing its connectedness to life, teachers may need to operate in the "teacher as midwife" mode promoted by Mary Belenky and her colleagues. In this mode, teachers recognize birthing ideas and nurse them along, knowing that ideas and persons grow with nurturing. They help students "deliver their words to the world" and expose them to voices of others with whom they can blend (219). Connected knowing is a form of learning "based on empathy, listening, and believing" (Kirsch 16). The most important role of educators is to lessen students' feelings of being outsiders by "validating and supporting" them with "social, intellectual, and emotional support" (Hayes and Flannery 77). If the women can use "their life experience as a source of intellectual inquiry, [they can] . . . locate their own experiences in a broader social and political context" (76). However, teachers also need to be aware that women learn in more diverse ways and that connectedness is a way of knowing for some men as well (Hayes and Flannery; Qualley; Kirsch). Beginning with regard for students in their classrooms, caregiving teachers become listeners and allow students to teach them. They are receptive, especially to adult students who are "already active and important participants in our culture's conversation" (Kiskis 68). Trusting in students' abilities and literacies, teachers actively engage them in creating their own knowledge.

Belenky and her colleagues' midwife role closely aligns with the approach to learning advocated by Carl Rogers, teachers as facilitators. These teachers set "the initial mood or climate," clarify class purposes, involve students in implementing class purposes, and provide the "widest possible range of resources for learning." As facilitators, they regard themselves as human resources and potential learners, share with the group, become aware of "expressions of deep or strong feelings," and remain willing to accept their own limitations (Knowles, Holton, and Swanson 85–86). In the classroom, students learn in a comfortable and trustworthy atmosphere where differences are accepted and responsibilities are shared (93–94).

More than young people, nontraditional students can be motivated to be good students if they know that education "helps them solve problems in their lives or results in internal payoffs . . . quality of life, satisfaction, and self-esteem" (Knowles, Holton, and Swanson 149). Adults are more self-directed, so the teacher who can provide opportunities for them to learn on their own will be rewarded. Life experience "plays a major role in shaping their learning," and new knowledge will fit into that prior knowledge. They need to buy into the learning process, believe in the authenticity of the project, and have opportunities to reflect on their knowledge (140–42). Educators need "to respond to differences in the motivation and learning processes of nontraditional-age students" with demonstrations of applications of learning to real life (Justice and Dornan 248). One of my case study participants, Jean, says that teachers who do not look down on students—who are able to communicate with and create a willingness to learn in students—motivate students like her and made all the difference between her early schooling and college (April 29, 1999).

The role of the caregiving teacher is one who "encourages women to participate in dialogical, collaborative, and democratic ways of teaching and learning" (S. Rodriguez 8). Once students perceive relationships with teachers with whom they can "shape their social reality and . . . [are] no longer isolated and powerless, they begin to participate in dialogue with a larger world, first orally and then through writing" (Elsasser and John-Steiner 361). For these women, the personal attention of their teachers available at small institutions like Preston College made their dialogue more possible.

As Activists

As teachers and members of the community ourselves, we need to work to change the inequities based on gender and class and link ourselves with "productive social movements that redress social inequities" (Heaney). The best means of social change is activating strengths of students and encouraging them to question what they are being taught, to recognize the gray areas of life, to think critically, and to continue on their journey of lifelong education. Then teachers can look to the "emergence of persons who can think for themselves, can commit to inquiry in place of absolutism, can construct a democratic society that acknowledges and honors diverse beliefs, opinions, and cultural activities" (K. Taylor 61). Finally, pushing beyond ethnocentric and cultural views of literacy, teachers might recognize the broader view of literacy as symbols and signs that help people make meaning in their lives (Neilsen); the classroom is just one place among many where that can happen. Hepzibah Roskelly encourages teachers to tell stories about "holding your own against the odds," a technique that for her is the "most effective way of creating active learners who make the connections, as well as my most effective way of reminding learners of who they are" (300). She wants students to "believe in institutions and fight them at the same time . . . so they won't lose their own voices" (303). Being aware of class differences and respecting the oral culture from which they come, teachers can encourage their students "to develop and trust their oral and literate ways while continuing to communicate the struggles entailed in being other-cultural and outside the middle-class" (Villanueva, *Bootstraps* 115).

Teachers can become advocates for working-class students by being aware of social class, for our "genuine concern for diversity should lead us to question the selective functions of the academy and the role of composition in maintaining them" (Soliday 731). Mary Soliday encourages those in the classroom to question gatekeeping policies and practices that continue to divide middle- and working-class students in the academy. Certainly, teaching in this manner will do more for students than merely passing along writing without politics. Writing program administrators particularly need to "contest the traditional selective functions that our programs may perform" such as skills testing, proficiency tests, and so on (739).

Implications for Colleges

Recruitment

Colleges need to recognize the potential of these nontraditional women and recruit other students like them. Despite the lack of job opportunities in education, these women felt resolute that the college gave them the gift of confidence and self-esteem. They felt that they gained life skills, blaming the job market and age discrimination for their inability to get work. Because they generally are more committed to finishing their degree and because they add value to the classroom and become role models for younger students (S. Rodriguez 7), nontraditional women are ideal to supplement declining college enrollments. These interviews also confirmed for me the importance of the small college setting for nontraditional students, so those institutions should capitalize on their strengths of smaller classes and teaching faculty.

Support Services

Because these women go to college for financial reasons, the college might work to keep them in college and increase their loyalty to the institution by lessening financial burdens, encouraging student involvement, and providing counseling and support services designed for each student (Billson and Terry). Colleges and universities serving this student population can provide better career counseling (Wilson and Christian), perhaps encouraging nontraditional students to have a backup selection of courses in case opportunities are not available in the major they choose. If colleges promote the idea that more education means better jobs, then they should make every effort not to turn out graduates to face unemployment or underemployment by helping students conduct more realistic job market searches. At the same time, colleges can continue to teach critical thinking and other broad-based skills to help students adjust to the changing employment world like Polly, Mary, and other women were able to do. Their adjustability to unknown circumstances and their ability to be easily trained made the difference between unemployment and employment.

By providing low-cost child care or referral; more lenient admissions policies (which might not only accept the GED but also waive the ACT or other standardized pre-admissions testing); work study and financial aid packages; and peer mentoring, tutoring, and counseling, colleges can attract and retain students like the Preston County women. In addition, colleges can provide in-service training for faculty not accustomed to teaching nontraditional students but who have a direct impact on these women's success (S. Rodriguez; Sundberg). Jeanne Wilson and Connie Christian advocate creating a "re-entry specialist" for these women, providing more grants and scholarships and offering more varied selection of programs and degrees. Colleges can also make the process of attending college less complicated by providing outreach to students. By educating these women, colleges "empower society" at the same time (S. Rodriguez 7–8).

Life Adjustments

Because these women frequently have to work to pay college costs and may have to care for family members, colleges need to provide chances for these nontraditional students to step in and out of the educational process. Research illustrates that working-class students rarely complete their course work in four years because of family and work conflicts, and they may "stop out" to raise children or care for family members (Sternglass). Though college promises upward mobility and education for all, we need to be aware of the struggles working-class students encounter and not create more barriers that belie our promise.

If a family member of a nontraditional student is ill part of the semester, or if these students have job pressures, teachers might be more patient with late assignments. If students have to drop out, the institution might perhaps give them credit for the work they have done to that point so that they do not come back to school empty-handed. Such policies would make it easier for them to re-enter when family circumstances stabilize. Distant learning opportunities and other creative alternatives to traditional classroom-based learning, such as online courses or interactive television, might also assist these women (Sundberg).

Writing Across the Curriculum and Beyond College

These graduates stated that they wrote in many other disciplines besides English. Particularly in their education classes, they wrote often and experimented in a variety of modes. Writing across the curriculum will prepare literate graduates who can express themselves well. Since women value the connection of learning to their lives, linking expository and workplace literacy skills by showing contrasts and purposes seems an obvious function of the college. Having graduates from different professions come to composition classes to illustrate the importance of writing beyond college might also help college freshmen of all ages see beyond enduring the English requirement to readying themselves for real-life literacy. To help students see this connection, college faculty in all disciplines can use writing "as a means of initiating students into a disciplinary or professional community" so they know what is expected within their professions (Sitler). Helen Sitler encourages educational practices that work to connect life and school settings so that "literacy and learning flourish because the academic and the rest of life [meet] at the edges and create a fertile learning environment" (255). Teachers can learn to be "more respectful of students' need to write job applications, church bulletins, and family newsletters, as well as their need to write academic essays. The 'real world' isn't necessarily 'less' than the academic world" (Bencich). Students can then make the transition from expository, academic writing in college to the kind of writing nurses and social workers, for example, do, affirming the value of each so that one is not privileged over the other.

Conclusion

While the stage on which these women acted out their literacy was located in the central Appalachian Mountains, the literacy stories of the Preston County women resemble those of other underrepresented groups everywhere who, when given the chance, overcome odds and build confidence to lift up themselves and their families. Academic literacy in the form of a college education enabled these strong and inherent survivors to build on the talents they brought to the classroom, overcoming objections of family, taking their new literacy and fitting it to their practical purposes and remaining in the place they call home.

Their voices crow in individual ways. Lucy roars that going to college was originally to prepare herself for a job, but "after I got into it, it got to be more for me, to make me feel better about ME" (April 22, 1999). Jean, passing on a legacy to her grandchildren, bellows that making a difference in her world would be "better than running for president" (April 29, 1999). Sarah's voice shouts: "I am bound and determined I will be successful" (May 4, 1999). They know that if they do not seek solutions to their problems, then those from the outside will step in (Bailey), as evidenced by the plethora of programs designed by missionaries and politicians since the late 1800s to shape this region into step with the rest of the country.

When I re-read the transcripts and case studies, I am made speechless by all that I didn't know and learned from these articulate, generous women. They gave me the most precious gift of time and generosity, riches that have touched me deeply. In their typical mountain politeness, they supplemented the knowledge I gathered during my doctoral program by making theory come to life. I thank them for the honor of their trust, and I hope that I have honored them with an accurate representation of them to make their whistlin' and crowin' voices reverberate throughout the land, for they have indeed come to good ends.

Appendixes

Works Cited

Index

Appendix A
Interview Questions,
January–February 1999

Literacy is defined as the use of symbol systems, most particularly, in our culture, reading and writing. In addition to reading books, newspapers, and magazines, we read and write shopping lists, junk mail, letters and cards, poems, diaries, songs, official letters, bills, forms, scrapbooks, recipes, address books, local newspapers, catalogs, ads, instructions for new products we buy. We take messages; we keep records, calendars, appointments. If we belong to a group, we read minutes, newsletters, notices. Watching TV, looking at the computer, helping children with homework, and researching family history are also considered literacy.

Pre-college
1. Before college, what sort of reading and writing did you and your family do?

2. Who or what most influenced you to come to college?

3. Were you the first in your family to attend?

College
1. When you were in college, how did you have to change your reading and writing habits? How did you have to change your way of thinking, of gathering knowledge? From freshman to senior year, what changes did you notice in yourself?

2. What was the most or the least helpful to you when you were in college?

3. Some of you expressed a fear that getting an education might cause problems in your family. Did that happen?

4. How did college affect your home life? I am particularly interested in the reactions of your children.

5. Reflect on the writing you did in my class.

Post-college

1. In my class, you expressed hopes and dreams. Tell me what has happened to those.

2. Tell me about what you've been doing since college. Describe the changes in you and in your life as a result of college. What might you be doing if you had not gone to college?

3. Do you feel that college adequately prepared you for what you have been doing since college?

4. What sort of reading and writing do you do on the job?

5. What sort of reading and writing do you do for yourself outside the job (novels, journals, letters to the editor, letters to friends)? How do these activities differ from your pre-college behavior?

6. If you are active in church, what sort of reading and writing goes on around you (church bulletins, sending cards to sick members, hymnals, prayer cards, etc.)?

7. What are the attitudes of your family toward reading and writing?

8. All things considered, evaluate your college experience.

9. Tell me about your family's literacy.

Appendix B
Questions for Family Members

1. Tell me about the time your family member was going to school. Why do you think she went back?

2. What was the immediate effect on you of this person returning to college? What was the immediate effect on your family? Did you change your attitude as she went through college? In what ways? How did other family members react?

3. What changes have you seen in this person from before college, through college, to now? In what ways has she stayed the same? In what ways has she changed?

4. Does this person use more reading and writing since she graduated from college? In what ways?

5. How does this person use reading and writing in the home? on the job? in the community (church, school, etc.)?

6. Do you think that going to college helped or hindered this person? Do you think your family member realized all the dreams that she had hoped for?

7. How do you feel about women getting a college education?

8. Tell me about the reading and writing you did growing up and now. This includes grocery lists, paying bills, writing letters or love notes, reading horoscopes and magazines, etc.

Appendix C
Final Case Study Interview Questions,
April–May 1999

I asked these questions to all three case study participants in addition to specific questions to supplement missing information from prior interview and participant observation.

1. How would you evaluate your high school experiences (academic and social)?

2. How did teachers treat you in the classroom in terms of your work, your language, your dress? Who were your role models in high school?

3. For someone who has never been here, how would you describe daily life in Preston County: religious life, your life, family life, school? What's positive and what could be improved about this place? What is important for people to know about this area?

4. In a normal work day, about what percentage of your work is spent on writing? reading?

5. Do you have any piece of writing that you would consider sharing with me? Do you have any papers from class? Did you ever publish anything?

6. How did you adjust after college—immediately, three months later, one year, two years, five years? Did you have any problems with identity?

7. What are your perceptions of what a literate person is? an illiterate person?

8. What way do you learn best (orally, hands-on, academically [lectures, etc.], visually)?

9. A. Do you, your children, and/or your spouse belong to organizations that send newsletters, magazines, minutes of meetings? If yes, list them. Give examples.

   B. Do you do any reading and writing in the community? For example, do you belong to a group (list) that takes minutes, has a newsletter, etc.?

10. What are the reasons that you chose Preston College over the local community college?

11. How have your reading/writing/computer skills changed since college? Do you use these skills for personal growth, job advancement, or social power?

12. Tell me about your use of the public library, public school, and college library throughout your life until the present.

13. What sort of books do you own (textbooks, novels, etc.)?

14. Do you feel that your college education has given you financial security? Does your husband draw disability? Or do you both depend on your salary?

15. Where, with whom, and when do/did you read and write? Do you have a special place for pens and paper and the like and actual writing?

16. When you approach a reading task (on the job or for pleasure), reflect on what your attitude is, why you are reading, what circumstances surround the reading, and how you use the information.

17. How do you exchange information with family, friends, co-workers, and supervisors?

18. Who/what challenges your mind now? Now that you are out of college, what inspires you?

19. Do you consider yourself more literate, more educated, than you were before college? How does that make you feel?

20. Do you feel that you achieved the hopes and dreams you set out to achieve?

21. What changes have occurred in your life as a result of higher education?

22. How have your reading/writing/computer habits changed since college? Compare your reading and writing in college to now.

23. A. Talk about something you have read recently—tell the story.

    B. Talk about something you have written recently.

    C. Would you have been able to do either of these activities—reading or writing—while in college?

24. How has college changed the way you think about yourself?

Appendix D
Marty and I

Voices from the Hill
Writing Program, Preston College, 1992–93

Lucy

Alex Mullins, a neighbor who lives about a fourth of a mile down the road from where we live, asked my brother and me to get a swarm of bumblebees out of his corncrib (a building used to store grain), in which they had made their home. The corncrib sat on a flat, in a field on the hillside just above his house. The bees had made their hive among some rotten boards that had been stored there. Although he hired us, he didn't think we could do the job. "I don't think you can do it, but you're sure welcome to try," he said with a chuckle. Just knowing that he didn't think we could do the job made us more determined to get the job done.

Marty and I then set out to do what Alex saw as an impossible task. First, we had to gather all the equipment we would need. We borrowed two mining hats from our uncle and some fishing nets to put over our heads and faces so that the bees couldn't sting us. Then we took a rake from the barn, a grabbling hook to pull the boards out of the crib, and we got our grandfather's bee smoke gun (a can with a tube coming from it that is connected to a hand-held pump that sucks the smoke from the can). My grandfather had used it many times when harvesting the honey from his beehives. We were now ready for the battle with the bees.

As we began up the hill and got closer to the crib, we could see the bumblebees flying in and out, and I began to have second thoughts. "Are you sure those bees won't sting us?" I asked nervously. "Sure, sure," Marty replied with confidence. Then we began putting on our gear. First, we put on the mining hats, and then we

179

stretched the fishing nets over our hats and faces; we were ready to begin the job.

Marty took the grabbling hook, hooking one board at a time, and pulled it out of the crib. The first board or two came out without any problems. As Marty pulled the boards out, I would rake out the straw and mud that the bees had used to make their home. After about the fourth board, we exposed the center of the hive, and that was when the real battle began. The bees were everywhere, filling the sky like a dark cloud.

"OH, MY GOD!!" Marty yelled as he grabbed the smoke gun and began puffing out the smoke towards the angry bumblebees, but there was no effect. Because the smoke wouldn't stop the bumblebees, soon all the bees were out of the corncrib and ready for war.

Then I felt the sharp, warm sting of a bee to my ear and to the back of my neck. I suddenly realized with horror that the bumblebees had gotten under my net. I began to scream in pain. "Help me, Marty! Help me! They're in my hat." "Hold still!" he yelled as he grabbed a horseweed out of the ground that was growing near the corncrib. By the time he got to me, I was halfway down the hill, and all my gear was lying on the hill behind me.

"They're in my hair! They're in my hair!" I screamed even louder in pain. Then he took the horseweed that he was holding and began to smack at me; he might have been aiming for my head, but my face received most of the blows. Although I had about a hundred knots on my head and my face was blood red with whelps, the job was done. The bumblebees were gone: when Marty was pulling out the boards, the queen bee had been squashed, and the worker bees wouldn't stay if they didn't have a queen.

And that is how Marty and I got rid of the bumblebees in Alex's corncrib. However, I'm not sure that the fifteen dollars we earned was worth the pain I had to endure. I'm not even sure the money covered the cost of the alcohol and medicated cream that I had to use on all my stings. But there is one thing for certain: the next time neighbors have bumblebee hives in the corncrib, they'd better learn to live with them. Because of this experience, the bee fighting days are definitely over for Marty and me.

Appendix E
Grandma's Chocolate Gravy

Voices from the Hill
Writing Program, Preston College, 1994–95

Jean

Last Saturday and Sunday turned out to be a very hectic weekend. I had unexpected out-of-town guests who came to visit. Saturday morning was unusually busy. I was trying to prepare enough breakfast to feed everyone. While I fixed the usual eggs, biscuits, sausage, and bacon, I also fixed chocolate gravy. One of my guests happened to be Allie, a ten-year-old. She had never heard of chocolate gravy. Her first reaction was, "Ooh, gross!" Her next question was, "How do you make it?"

As I explained to her, "This is a recipe that I will never forget. You have to taste chocolate gravy to appreciate it. Watch carefully. I will take you through the steps my grandmother went through."

Chocolate gravy is an old family recipe of my grandma's. When I was young, I would stay with her for a week at a time. During this period, she would make chocolate gravy for me. I considered that the ultimate breakfast of all. I looked forward to staying with her and even to getting up in the morning.

"Allie," I said; "I still remember the conversation my grandmother and I would have every morning. My grandmother would walk into the bedroom and say, 'Jean, it is time to get up. Come and eat your breakfast. I have to go milk the cow.' I would reply in a low voice, 'Not right now; I want to sleep just a little bit longer.' Then as she turned to go out of the bedroom, she would say, 'I made chocolate gravy. You'd better get it while it's hot.' Those were the magic words—'CHOCOLATE GRAVY.' Before she got to the kitchen, I was right behind her."

"Sometimes I would get to sit and watch my grandma go through the steps to make chocolate gravy. She would use these ingredients: 1 ½ cups sugar, 4 tablespoons flour, 4 tablespoons cocoa, ½ cup milk. First, she would combine the sugar, flour, and cocoa in a bowl, making sure they were all mixed together. Then, she would pour the dry ingredients into a cooker on the stove. Next, Grandma would add the milk and water, stirring until thoroughly mixed. She placed the cooker on medium heat until it started to boil. Grandma would stir the mixture until it was just right, making sure not to let it scorch."

"Finally, she would take it off the heat and pour it into a bowl. I would always take one of her homemade biscuits and tear it apart, placing it on the plate. Grandma would take a spoonful of chocolate gravy and pour it over the biscuit. Then she would top it with butter to my satisfaction."

Grandma's chocolate gravy is not only a very special recipe to me, but also holds sentimental meaning. When I think of chocolate gravy, I see myself with my grandmother, sitting in her warm kitchen in the early morning hours eating breakfast. As I explained to Allie, "This is a special recipe that is passed from one generation to the next."

Appendix F
Looks Can Be Deceiving

Voices from the Hill
Writing Program, Preston College, 1990–91

Sarah

Each night millions of Americans watch TV for entertainment. When a program introduces us to a different section of the world, it captures our attention because we want to know what other areas are like and how they differ from our own environment. In a recent production of *48 Hours,* the producer's crew interviewed and visited some of the people of Floyd County in Eastern Kentucky.

During an interview with the Johnson family from Muddy Gut holler, the interviewer repeatedly asked, "Why don't you leave this place?" The response from the Johnson family was that they did not want to split their family apart. This is not necessarily typical of Appalachians. Many people feel close to their families but do move away for one reason or another. For example, I was brought up in a holler called Big Hackney's Creek. After I married Bill, we moved to Johns Creek to be near his job. Bill is a truck driver, and our living closer to his job makes it easier for him. We have made Johns Creek home for now. My Aunt Shelia grew up in the head of Grapevine. After her divorce, Shelia and her three kids moved to Florida, because she is an LPN and the wages are better there. She has made Florida home until something better comes her way. My friend Pamela was raised in a holler called Hen Roost. After she married her husband, Frank, she moved to West Germany. Frank is in the United States Air Force and is stationed there for three years. Germany will be Pamela's home until it is time to move again.

Next, the program displayed several different houses. They were small, usually with only a couple of rooms, and only half completed.

They suggested that Appalachians live in mere shacks. There are people who actually live this way, but there are many people who do not. For instance, my mom lives at Big Hackney's Creek in a six-room house that has a basement and a carport. My in-laws live at Grapevine in a mobile home. They have remodeled their trailer, and now it is considered a six-room house. My uncle, who lives at Meathouse a few houses above me, lives in a beautiful brick house that has eight rooms. He also has a carport and a paved driveway.

Finally, the program showed a young couple getting married. Before the ceremony took place, the interviewer talked with the bride and groom. The couple talked about how excited they were about getting married and later having babies. This portrayal implied that all the young people of Eastern Kentucky are hillbillies who just want to hurry and get married at an early age and have babies. Sure, there are many young people who do get married and start a family immediately, but that happens everywhere. This does not mean that all Eastern Kentuckians marry by the time they are eighteen years old. For example, I did not marry Bill until I was twenty years old. My friend Tara was twenty-eight years old before she married her husband Jason, and she did not have her first child until she was thirty. My Aunt Drew is forty years old and is still a single lady today. She says she hasn't found the right man yet.

Even though the different situations that *48 Hours* exposed are here, this does not mean that one small area represents Eastern Kentucky as a whole. We do have people who do not want to leave, no matter what. We do have our poor communities. We are considered hillbillies because we live in the mountains, but the crew from *48 Hours* showed the rest of America only what they wanted them to see. Gosh, can't looks be deceiving?

Appendix G
Lucy's Letters to the Editor

Appalachian News-Express
November 20, 2002

DO NOT MAKE CUTS IN EDUCATION FUND

Good morning, good afternoon or good evening, whichever time you are reading this. I have awakened once again with a pet peeve— I guess they seem to come more often these days. But as most of you have heard, there is a pending education fund cut for the up and coming new year. I know you are sitting there in amazement at this news . . . not!

It just seems to me that anytime there is a budget cut the education of our children is the first to suffer. Let's examine this a bit closer. Our government is expecting our school systems to be proficient by the year 2014. How is this to be accomplished with a school funding cut each year?

I challenge our state government to become proficient. Its ineptitude has drained our surplus and now our children are to be the ones to suffer, as well as newly graduating teachers seeking employment in a system that can not support their needs.

It seems to me that if there is to be budget-cutting, the best place to start would be for our lawmakers to not start off the new year with a pay raise for themselves.

Don't let our state government stay at the novice level. Come on boys, catch up to our school systems.

Appalachian News-Express
March 19, 2004

PLEASE HELP EDUCATE ABOUT CYSTIC FIBROSIS

Below you will find the Internet link to a letter to request that the month of May be set as Cystic Fibrosis Awareness Month.

This is very personal to me because my daughter has cystic fibrosis and the need to educate the public is great. This reality hit home just a few weeks ago after recently she had a flare-up and had to miss a week of school. She was so glad to get back to school to see her friends. But upon returning to school it was not so happy. Some of the kids wouldn't talk or play with her and the ones who did weren't nice. They said things to her like, "I can't play with you. My mom said you would make me sick," "I'll get sick and have to go to the hospital if I get around you," and I can never forget this one, a boy classmate told her, "My mom said I can't get around you and if I do she will know because she can smell you on me." I cannot begin to explain the anger I felt and the utter shock.

Please if you will take the time to write your representative and ask him or her to vote yes on this important issue. Letters must be in by Monday. Please if you can mail or fax the letter to Jim Bunning at 316 Hart Senate Office Building, Washington, DC 20510-1703. You can call Bunning at 202/224-4343 or fax the letter to 202/228-1373.

The letter can be found at www.cff.org/legislative_action/.

Thank you for your time and caring.

Works Cited

Anglin, Mary. "A Question of Loyalty: National and Regional Identity in Narratives of Appalachia." *Anthropological Quarterly* 65.3 (1992): 115–16.

Aronson, Anne. "Reversals of Fortune: Downward Mobility and the Writing of
Nontraditional Students." Linkon 39–55.

Ashley, Hannah. "Playing the Game: Proficient Working-Class Students Writers'
Second Voices." *Research in the Teaching of English* 35.4 (2001): 493–524.

Bailey, Bennie R. "Appalachia: Our Home." Speech, opening convocation, Preston
College, Preston, KY. Fall 1998.

Barton, David, and Mary Hamilton. *Local Literacies: Reading and Writing in One
Community.* London: Routledge, 1998.

Batteau, Allen W. *The Invention of Appalachia.* Tucson: U of Arizona P, 1990.

Belenky, Mary Field, et al. *Women's Ways of Knowing: The Development of Self,
Voice, and Mind.* New York: Basic, 1997.

Belenky, Mary Field, Lynne A. Bond, and Jacqueline S. Weinstock. *A Tradition
That Has No Name: Nurturing the Development of People, Families, and
Communities.* New York: Basic, 1997.

Bencich, Carole. Personal interview. July 1999.

Billings, Dwight B., and Kathleen M. Blee. *The Road to Poverty: The Making of
Wealth and Hardship in Appalachia.* Cambridge: Cambridge UP, 2000.

Billings, Dwight B., Guerney Norman, and Katherine Ledford. *Confronting
Appalachian Stereotypes.* Lexington: UP of Kentucky, 1999.

Billson, J. M., and M. B. Terry. "In Search of the Silken Purse: Factors in Attri-
tion among First-Generation Students." *College and University* 58.1
(1982): 57–75.

Bingman, Mary Beth. "Women in Appalachian Community Organizations: Sites
of Learning and Change." *Journal of Appalachian Studies* 5.2 (1999): 215–
26.

Bishop, Wendy. *Ethnographic Writing Research: Writing It Down, Writing It Up,
and Reading It.* Portsmouth, NH: Heinemann, 1999.

Bissex, Glenda. *Partial Truths: A Memoir and Essays on Reading, Writing, and
Researching.* Portsmouth, NH: Heinemann, 1996.

Bizzell, Patricia. *Academic Discourse and Critical Consciousness.* Pittsburgh: U
of Pittsburgh P, 1992.

Boone, Elizabeth, and Walter Mignolo. *Writing Without Words: Alternative
Literacies in Mesoamerica and the Andes.* Durham, NC: Duke UP, 1994.

Boulding, Elise. *Women in the Twentieth Century World*. New York: Wiley, 1977.

Brandau, Deborah. *Literacy and Literature in School and Non-School Settings*. Report Series 7.6. Albany, NY: National Research Center on English Learning and Achievement. ERIC, 1996. ED 401 550.

Brandt, Deborah. "Accumulating Literacy: Writing and Learning to Write in the Twentieth Century." *College English* 57.6 (1995): 649–68.

———. *Literacy in American Lives*. Cambridge: Cambridge UP, 2001.

Briscoe, Lori, et al. "Unruly Woman: An Interview with Helen Lewis." *Appalachian Journal* 27.2 (2000): 164–89.

Brooke, Robert E., ed. *Rural Voices: Place-Conscious Education and the Teaching of Writing*. New York: Teachers College P, 2003.

———. *Writing and Sense of Self: Identity Negotiation in Writing Workshops*. Urbana, IL: NCTE, 1991.

Brooks, Ann K. "Transformation." Hayes and Flannery 139–53.

Caudill, Kelli, and Charity Quillen. *Searching for an Appalachian Accent*. Whitesburg, KY: Appalshop, 2002.

Chiseri-Strater, Elizabeth, and Bonnie Sunstein. *FieldWorking: Reading and Writing Research*. Upper Saddle River, NJ: Blair, 1997.

Cintron, Ralph. *Angels' Town: Chero Ways, Gang Life, and Rhetorics of the Everyday*. Boston: Beacon, 1997.

Cushman, Ellen. *The Struggle and the Tools: Oral and Literate Strategies in an Inner City Community*. Albany: State U of New York P, 1998.

Daniell, Beth. *A Communion of Friendship: Literacy and Women's Spiritual Practice in Al-Anon*. Carbondale: Southern Illinois UP, 2003.

———. "Narratives of Literacy: Connecting Composition to Culture." *College Composition and Communication* 50.3 (1999): 393–410.

DeRosier, Linda Scott. *Creeker: A Woman's Journey*. Lexington: UP of Kentucky, 1999.

Donehower, Kimberley K. *Beliefs about Literacy in a Southern Appalachian Community*. Diss. University of Minnesota, 1997. Ann Arbor: UMI, 1997. 9738422.

———. "Literacy Choices in an Appalachian Community." *Journal of Appalachian Studies* 9.2 (2003): 341–62.

———. "Re: thanks." E-mail to the author. Jan. 27, 2003.

Dorgan, Howard. *The Old Regular Baptists of Central Appalachia: Brothers and Sisters in Hope*. Knoxville: U of Tennessee P, 1989.

Edwards, J., and H. Giles. "Applications of the Social Psychology of Language: Sociolinguistics and Education." *Applied Linguistics*. Ed. Peter Trudgill. London: Academic, 1984. 119–58.

Egan, Marcia. "Appalachian Women: The Path from the 'Hollers' to Higher Education." *Affilia* 8.3 (1993): 265–76.

Elsasser, N., and V. P. John-Steiner. "An Interactionist Approach to Advancing Literacy." *Harvard Educational Review* 47.3 (1977): 355–69.

Ferretti, Eileen. "Between Dirty Dishes and Polished Discourse: How Working-Class Moms Construct School Identities." Linkon 69–84.

Fiene, Judith. "The Social Reality of a Group of Rural, Low-Status, Appalachian Women: A Grounded Theory Study." Diss. University of Tennessee, Knoxville, 1988.

Financial Aid Office, Pikeville College. Telephone interview. Sept. 9, 1999.

Flynn, Elizabeth A. "Composing as a Woman." *Crosstalk in Comp Theory: A Reader.* Ed. Victor Villanueva. Urbana, IL: NCTE, 1997. 549–64.

Gee, James Paul. *Social Linguistics and Literacies: Ideologies in Discourses.* 2d ed. London: Taylor and Mary, 1996.

Geissenger, C., et al. "Rural Women and Isolation: Pathways to Reconnection." *Affilia* 8.3 (1993): 277–99.

Giesen, Carol A. B. *Coal Miners' Wives: Portraits of Endurance.* Lexington: UP of Kentucky, 1995.

Goodman, Ken. *On Reading: A Common-Sense Look at the Nature of Language and the Science of Reading.* Portsmouth, NH: Heinemann, 1996.

Graber, Elizabeth. Personal interview. Mar. 21, 2003.

Guba, E. G., and Y. S. Lincoln. *Effective Evaluation.* San Francisco: Jossey-Bass, 1981.

Guerra, Juan. *Close to Home: Oral and Literate Practices in a Transnational Mexicano Community.* New York: Teachers College/Columbia UP, 1998.

Gutwein, Geri. Personal communication. Mar. 25, 2003.

Hamilton, Sharon Jean. *My Name's Not Susie: A Life Transformed by Literacy.* Portsmouth, NH: Boynton/Cook Heinemann, 1995.

Hammons-Bryner, S. "Interpersonal Relationships and African American Women's Educational Achievement: An Ethnographic Study." *SAGE* 9.1 (1995): 10–17.

Hanna, Stephen. "Representation and the Reproduction of Appalachian Space: A History of Contested Signs and Meanings." *Historical Geography* 28 (2000): 179–207.

Harrienger, M. "Writing a Life: The Composing of Grace." *Feminine Principles and Women's Experiences in American Composition and Rhetoric.* Ed. Louise W. Phelps and Janet W. Emig. Pittsburgh: U of Pittsburgh P, 1995. 137–52.

Hartwell, Patrick. "Dialect Interference in Writing: A Critical View." *Research in the Teaching of Writing* 14 (1980): 101–18.

Hayes, Elisabeth. "Social Contexts." Hayes and Flannery 23–52.

———. "Voice." Hayes and Flannery 79–110.

Hayes, Elisabeth, and Daniele D. Flannery, eds.. *Women as Learners: The Significance of Gender in Adult Learning.* San Francisco: Jossey-Bass, 2000.

Heaney, Thomas W. *Learning to be Heard: Organization, Power and Literacy.* National-Louis University. Faculty papers. July 30, 1995 <http://www3. nl.edu/academics/cas/ace/facultypapers/ThomasHeaney_Learning.cfm>.

Heath, Shirley B. "Protean Shapes in Literacy Events: Ever-Shifting Oral and Literate Traditions." *Spoken and Written Language: Exploring Orality and Literacy.* Ed. Deborah Tannen. Norwood, NJ: Ablex, 1982.

———. *Ways with Words: Language, Life, and Work in Communities and Class-rooms.* Cambridge: Cambridge UP, 1983.

Horsman, Jennifer. *Something in My Mind Besides the Everyday: Women and Literacy.* Toronto: Women's, 1990.

Hymes, Dell. *Ethnography, Linguistics, Narrative Inequality: Toward an Under-standing of Voice.* London: Taylor and Francis, 1996.

Isserman, Lawrence. "Overview." *Socio-economic Review of Appalachia: Appa-lachia Then and Now: An Update of "The Realities of Deprivation" Reported to the President in 1964.* Ed. Andrew M. Isserman. Washington, DC: Ap-palachian Regional Commission, 1996. 1–30.

Jones, Loyal. *Appalachian Values.* Ashland, KY: Jesse Stuart Foundation, 1994.

———. *Faith and Meaning in the Southern Uplands.* Urbana: U of Illinois P, 1999.

Justice, Elaine M., and Teresa M. Dornan. "Metacognitive Differences between Traditional-Age and Nontraditional-Age College Students." *Adult Educa-tion Quarterly* 51.3 (2001): 236–49.

Kahn, Kathy. *Hillbilly Women.* New York: Avon, 1972.

Keizer, Garret. *No Place but Here: A Teacher's Vocation in a Rural Community.* Hanover, NH: UP of New England, 1996.

Kendrick, Leatha. Letter to the author. Jan. 25, 2003.

Kentucky Information Page. "Population Change in Kentucky's 120 Counties: 1960–2000." Nov. 4, 2004 <http://www.louisville.edu/~easchn01/kentucky/ kypop1.htm>.

Kentucky State Data Center. *Persons 18 and Older by Gender and Educational Attainment.* Louisville: U of Louisville P, 1990.

Kirsch, Gesa. *Women Writing the Academy: Audience, Authority, and Transforma-tion.* Carbondale: Southern Illinois UP, 1993.

Kirsch, Gesa, and Peter Mortensen. *Ethics and Representation in Qualitative Studies of Literacy.* Urbana, IL: NCTE, 1996.

Kiskis, M. "Adult Learners, Autobiography, and Educational Planning: Reflec-tions on Pedagogy, Andragogy, and Power." Sullivan and Qualley 56–72.

Knowles, M. S., E. F. Holton, and R. A. Swanson. *The Adult Learner.* 5th ed. Houston, TX: Gulf, 1998.

Knox, W. E., P. Lindsay, and M. N. Kolb. *Does College Make a Difference? Long-Term Changes in Activities and Attitudes.* Westport, CT: Greenwood, 1993.

Knudson, Candy. Letter to the author. July 3, 1999.

Labov, William. *Language in the Inner City: Studies in Black English Vernacular.* Philadelphia: U of Pennsylvania P, 1972.

Lauer, Janice. Foreword. *My Name's Not Susie: A Life Transformed by Literacy.* By Sharon Jean Hamilton. Portsmouth, NH: Boynton/Cook, 1995.

Law, Carolyn Leste. Introduction. *This Fine Place So Far from Home: Voices of Academics from the Working-Class.* Ed. C. L. Barney Dews and Carolyn Leste Law. Philadelphia: Temple UP, 1995.

Lillis, Theresa M. *Student Writing: Access, Regulation, Desire.* London: Routledge, 2001.

Lincoln, Y. S., and E. G. Guba. *Naturalistic Inquiry.* Newbury Park, CA: Sage, 1985.

Linkon, Sherry Lee. *Teaching Working-Class.* Amherst, MA: U of Massachusetts P, 1999.

Lu, Min-Zhan. "An Essay on the Work of Composition: Composing English against the Order of Fast Capitalism." *College Composition and Communication* 56.1 (2004): 16–50.

Luhman, Reid. "Appalachian English Stereotypes: Language Attitudes in Kentucky." *Language in Society* 19 (1990): 331–48.

Lunneborg, Patricia W. *OU Women: Undoing Educational Obstacles.* London: Cassell, 1994.

Luttrell, Wendy. *Schoolsmart and Motherwise: Working-Class Women's Identity and Schooling.* New York: Routledge, 1997.

Lyon, Georgia Ella. "Voiceplace." *Bloodroot: Reflections on Place by Appalachian Women Writers.* Ed. Joyce Dyer. Lexington: UP of Kentucky, 1998. 167–74.

Maddox, Ed, and Connie Maddox. *Pike County, Kentucky: A Pictorial History.* Virginia Beach, VA: Donning, 1999.

Maggard, Sally. "Coalfield Women Making History." Billings, Norman, and Ledford 228–50.

McAndrew, Donald. Class notes. Summer 1997.

McCauley, Deborah. *Appalachian Mountain Religion: A History.* Urbana: U of Illinois P, 1995.

McNeil, W. K. *Appalachian Images in Folk and Popular Culture.* Ann Arbor, MI: UMI Research, 1989.

Merrifield, Juliet, et al. *Life at the Margins: Literacy, Language, and Technology in Everyday Life.* New York: Teachers College, 1997.

Milroy, J., and L. Milroy. *Authority in Language: Investigating Language Prescription and Standardisation.* London: Routledge, 1991.

Montgomery, Michael. "Myths: How a Hunger for Roots Shapes Our Notions about Appalachian English." *Now and Then: The Appalachian Magazine* 17.2 (2000): 7–13.

Neilsen, Lorri. *Literacy and Living: The Literate Lives of Three Adults.* Portsmouth, NH: Heinemann, 1989.

Newkirk, Thomas. "The Narrative Roots of the Case Study." *Research Methods and Methodology.* Ed. G. Kirsch and P. A. Sullivan. Carbondale: Southern Illinois UP, 1992. 130–52.

Obiols, Marina Solís. *The Matched Guise Technique: A Classic Test for Formal Measurement of Language Attitudes.* 2002. *Noves SL* <http://www6.gencat.net/llengcat/noves/hm02estiu/metodologia/a_solis1_5.htm>.

Okawa, Gail. "'Resurfacing Roots': Developing a Pedagogy of Language Awareness from Two Views." *Language Diversity in the Classroom: From Intention to Practice.* Ed. Geneva Smitherman and Victor Villanueva. Carbondale: Southern Illinois UP, 2003. 109–33.

Pagnucci, Gian. *Living the Narrative Life: Stories as a Tool for Meaning Making.* Portsmouth, NH: Heinemann, 2004.

Pari, Caroline. "'Just American': Reversing Ethnic and Class Assimilation in the Academy." Linkon 123–41.

Pascall, Gillian, and Roger Cox. *Women Returning to Higher Education.* London: Open UP, 1993.

Pascarella, Ernest T., and Patrick T. Terenzini. *How College Affects Students: Findings and Insights from Twenty Years of Research.* San Francisco: Jossey-Bass, 1991.

Pascarella, Ernest T., Gregory C. Wolniak, Christopher T. Pierson, and Patrick T. Terenzini. "Appalachian Region Alumni Outcomes Survey (Preliminary Findings)." Appalachian College Association. June 15, 2004 <acaweb.org>.

Piper, Deborah. "Psychology's Class Blindness: Investment in the Status Quo." *This Fine Place So Far from Home: Voices of Academics from the Working-Class.* Ed. C. L. Barney Dews and Carolyn Leste Law. Philadelphia: Temple UP, 1995. 286–96.

Price, Michael, Martye Scobee, and Thomas Sawyer. "Kentucky Migration: Consequences for State Population and Labor Force." Feb. 2004. University of Louisville Urban Studies Institute. <http://ksdc.louisville.edu/kpr/migration/kentucky_migration.pdf>.

Puckett, Anita. "'Let the Girls Do the Spelling and Dan Will Do the Shooting': Literacy, the Division of Labor, and Identity in a Rural Appalachian Community." *Anthropological Quarterly* 65.3 (1992): 137–47.

———. *Seldom Ask, Never Tell: Labor and Discourse in Appalachia.* Oxford: Oxford UP, 2000.

Purcell-Gates, Victoria. *Other People's Words: The Cycle of Low Literacy.* Cambridge: Harvard UP, 1997.

Qualley, D. J. "Being Two Places at Once: Feminism and the Development of 'Both/And' Perspectives." Sullivan and Qualley 25–42.

Reinharz, Shulamit. *Feminist Methods in Social Research.* New York: Oxford UP, 1992.

Rennick, Robert. "Pike County." *The Kentucky Encyclopedia.* Ed. J. E. Kleber. Lexington: UP of Kentucky, 1992. 721–22.

Rodriguez, Richard. *A Hunger for Memory: The Education of Richard Rodriguez: An Autobiography.* Boston: Godine, 1982.

Rodriguez, Sandra. "Detour from Nowhere: The Remarkable Journey of a Reentry College Woman." *Initiatives* 58.1 (1996): 1–10.

Rose, Mike. *Lives on the Boundary: A Moving Account of the Struggles and Achievements of America's Educational Underclass.* New York: Penguin, 1989.

Roskelly, Hepzibah. "Telling Tales in School." *Working-Class Women in the Academy: Laborers in the Knowledge Factory.* Ed. M. M. Tokarczyk and E. A. Fay. Amherst: U of Massachusetts P, 1993. 292–307.

Rotkis, J., and N. McDaniel. "Creating a Special Place in the Community College for Unique Students." *Community College Journal of Research and Practice* 17.4 (1993): 315–23.

Rowbotham, S. "What Do Women Want? Women-Centered Values and the World as It Is." *Feminist Review* 20 (1985): 49–69.

Seitz, Virginia. *Women, Development, and Communities for Empowerment in Appalachia.* Albany: State U of New York P, 1995.

Shapiro, Henry D. *Appalachia on Our Mind: The Southern Mountaineers in the American Consciousness, 1870–1920.* Chapel Hill: U of North Carolina P, 1978.

Shelby, Anne. "The 'R' Word: What's So Funny (and Not So Funny) about Redneck Jokes." Billings, Norman, and Ledford 153–60.

Shiber, John. "Nontraditional Students: The Importance of Getting There." *Innovation Abstract* 32.11 (1999): 1–2.

Shor, Ira. *When Students Have Power: Negotiating Authority in Critical Pedagogy.* Chicago: U of Chicago P, 1996.

Sitler, Helen. "Edge Effect Learning Zones: Literacies of School, Work, and Home in Dialogue Journals and Class Discussion." Diss. Indiana University of Pennsylvania, 1997.

Smith, Herb E. Personal communication. May 5, 2001.

Smithwick, W. K. "Description of Services." *Baptist Children's Messenger* 27.1 (1999): 11.

Soliday, Mary. "Class Dismissed." *College English* 61.6 (1999): 731–41.

Spellmeyer, Kurt. "Nothing You Do Will Make You Real: On the Limits of Identity Politics." Speech, 2002 Thomas R. Watson Conference, Louisville, KY. Oct. 10–12, 2002.

St. Clair's Bottom District Primitive Baptist Association. Apr. 7, 1999 <http://members.aol.com/jweaver303/pb/scb.htm>.

Sterling-Deer, Carolyn. Personal interview. Mar. 21, 2003.

Sternglass, Marilyn. *Time to Know Them.* Mahwah, NJ: Lawrence Erlbaum, 1977.

Still, James. *From the Mountain Valley: New and Collected Poems.* Ed. Ted Olson. Lexington: UP of Kentucky, 2001.

Street, Brian V. *Literacy and Development: Ethnographic Perspectives.* London: Routledge, 2001.

———. *Literacy in Theory and Practice.* Cambridge: Cambridge UP, 1984.

Stuckey, J. Elspeth. *The Violence of Literacy.* Portsmouth, NH: Heinemann, 1991.

Sullivan, P. A., and D. J. Qualley, eds. *Pedagogy in the Age of Politics: Writing and Reading (in) the Academy.* Urbana, IL: NCTE, 1994.

Sundberg, Elle. "Investigating the Nontraditional Student in the University System of Georgia: Enrollment Patterns." Summer 2001. June 2005 <http://ksumail.kennesaw.edu/~bkarcher/3_part_Investigating.htm>.

Taylor, D., and C. Dorsey-Gaines. *Growing up Literate: Learning from Inner-City Families.* Portsmouth, NH: Heinemann, 1988.

Taylor, K. "Why Psychological Models of Adult Development Are Important for the Practice of Adult Education: A Response to Courtenay." *Adult Education Quarterly* 46.4 (1996): 54–62.

Trudgill, Peter. *Sociolinguistics: An Introduction to Language and Society.* London: Penguin, 1995.

Vanderbrake, Katie. Personal interview. Dec. 11, 2002.

———. "Re: ACA Summit." E-mail to the author. Nov. 7, 2004.

Villanueva, Victor. *Bootstraps: An Academic of Color.* Urbana, IL: NCTE, 1993.

———. "Cuentos de mi Historia: An Art of Memory." *Personal Effects: The Social Character of Scholarly Writing.* Ed. Deborah Holdstein and David Bleich. Provo: Utah UP, 2001. 267–76.

———. Personal communication. Aug. 2000–Mar. 2003.

Walls, D. E. *The Kidwells: A Family Odyssey.* Durham, NC: Carolina Academic Press, 1983.

Wax, Murray L. "Knowledge, Power, and Ethics in Qualitative Social Research." *American Sociologist* 26.2 (1995): 22–35.

Whisnant, David E. *All That Is Native and Fine: The Politics of Culture in an American Region.* Chapel Hill: U of North Carolina P, 1983.

Wilson, Jeanne, and Connie Christian. "Career Development Needs of Re-entry Women in Appalachian Kentucky." Unpublished manuscript, 1986.

Wood, Lawrence, and Gregory A. Bischak. *Progress and Challenges in Reducing Economic Distress in Appalachia: An Analysis of National and Regional Trends since 1960.* Washington, DC: Appalachian Regional Commission, 2000.

Index

KATHERINE KELLEHER SOHN is an assistant professor of English at Pikeville College, where she teaches composition and coordinates the Writing Center. In addition to making numerous presentations to the Conference on College Composition and Communication, the Appalachian Studies Association, and the Appalachian College Association, she has published articles in *College Composition and Communication;* a book review for *Nantahala,* an on-line literary magazine; and a chapter for *Multiple Literacies for the Twenty-First Century,* edited by Huot, Stroble, and Bazerman. In 2001, Sohn received the James Berlin Outstanding Dissertation of the Year Award for her dissertation on which this book is based, "Whistlin' and Crowin' Women of Appalachia: Literacy Development since College."

Other Books in the Studies in Writing & Rhetoric Series

African American Literacies Unleashed: Vernacular English and the Composition Classroom
Arnetha F. Ball and Ted Lardner

Rhetoric and Reality: Writing Instruction in American Colleges, 1900–1985
James A. Berlin

Writing Instruction in Nineteenth-Century American Colleges
James A. Berlin

Something Old, Something New: College Writing Teachers and Classroom Change
Wendy Bishop

The Variables of Composition: Process and Product in a Business Setting
Glenn J. Broadhead and Richard C. Freed

Audience Expectations and Teacher Demands
Robert Brooke and John Hendricks

Archives of Instruction: Nineteenth-Century Rhetorics, Readers, and Composition Books in the Unites States
Jean Ferguson Carr, Stephen L. Carr, and Lucille M. Schultz

Rehearsing New Roles: How College Students Develop as Writers
Lee Ann Carroll

Dialogue, Dialectic, and Conversation: A Social Perspective on the Function of Writing
Gregory Clark

Toward a Grammar of Passages
Richard M. Coe

A Communion of Friendship: Literacy, Spiritual Practice, and Women in Recovery
Beth Daniell

Embodied Literacies: Imageword and a Poetics of Teaching
Kristie S. Fleckenstein

Writing with Authority: Students' Roles as Writers in Cross-National Perspective
David Foster

Writing Groups: History, Theory, and Implications
Anne Ruggles Gere

Sexuality and the Politics of Ethos in the Writing Classroom
Zan Meyer Gonçalves

Computers & Composing: How the New Technologies Are Changing Writing
Jeanne W. Halpern and Sarah Liggett

Teaching Writing as a Second Language
Alice S. Horning

Revisionary Rhetoric, Feminist Pedagogy, and Multigenre Texts
Julie Jung

Women Writing the Academy: Audience, Authority, and Transformation
Gesa E. Kirsch

Invention as a Social Act
Karen Burke LeFevre

A New Perspective on Cohesion in Expository Paragraphs
Robin Bell Markels

Response to Reform: Composition and the Professionalization of Teaching
Margaret J. Marshall

Gender Influences: Reading Student Texts
Donnalee Rubin

The Young Composers: Composition's Beginnings in Nineteenth-Century Schools
Lucille M. Schultz

Multiliteracies for a Digital Age
Stuart A. Selber

Technology and Literacy in the Twenty-First Century: The Importance of Paying Attention
Cynthia L. Selfe